Research in Labor Problems in the
United States

Studies in Labor

CONSULTING EDITOR: HENRY DAVID,
DIVISION OF BEHAVIORAL SCIENCES / NATIONAL ACADEMY
OF SCIENCES—NATIONAL RESEARCH COUNCIL

Research in
Labor Problems
in the
United States

Milton Derber

INSTITUTE OF LABOR AND INDUSTRIAL
RELATIONS / UNIVERSITY OF ILLINOIS

RANDOM HOUSE New York

To Zel

FIRST PRINTING

© *Copyright, 1967, by Random House, Inc.*
All rights reserved under International and Pan-American Copy-
right Conventions. Published in New York by Random House,
Inc. and simultaneously in Toronto, Canada, by Random House
of Canada Limited.
Library of Congress Catalog Card Number: 67–20620
Manufactured in the United States of America.
Composed by The Haddon Craftsmen, Inc., Scranton, Pa.
Printed by Halliday Lithograph Corp., West Hanover, Mass.
Bound by H. Wolff, New York, N. Y.
Typography by Leon Bolognese.

Foreword

The research literature discussed in this book is entirely American. This is a regrettable limitation because important contributions to labor research have been made by scholars in other countries, particularly Britain, France, and Germany, and interest in the field appears to be growing in such widely separated lands as Australia, India, Italy, Japan, and the Netherlands, not to mention the Soviet Union, Poland, and Yugoslavia among the Communist countries. Moreover, in addition to the writings in English, translations are making some of the more interesting foreign-language writings more accessible to the American student—the works of Georges Friedmann, Ralf Dahrendorf, and Jacques Ellul are illustrative.

The decision to confine the book to American sources was based on three considerations. First, limitations of space, which make it impossible to do full justice even to the American literature. Second, the limitations of the author's knowledge of the foreign literature. Finally, the still unresolved question of the applicability and interchangeability of concepts and findings as among the different culture areas of the world, which makes a merger of foreign and American literature difficult.

Despite the limitations noted above, the scope of this book is so wide that no one individual can hope to be expert on all of its aspects. I have benefited greatly from the advice and criticisms of colleagues and friends whose knowledge about special topics is much more thorough than my own. Obviously, any omissions or errors are entirely my responsibility. I am particularly indebted to the following: Harry M. Douty, Walter Franke, Joseph Gusfield, Melvin Rothbaum, Vladimir Stoikov, Adolf Sturmthal, and Harry Triandis. Mrs. Barbara Dennis gave me valuable editorial comments and prepared the Index.

Milton Derber

Contents

Foreword

I   *The Domain of Labor Problems Research*   3

II   *Origins in Reformism*   21

III   *Research as an Instrument of Administration*   37

IV   *Toward the Development of a Science*   56

V   *Expanding Knowledge and Current Gaps*   71

VI   *Methodological Problems*   111

VII   *Prospects for the Future*   140

Appendix: 159
Outline of an Introductory Research Course

NOTES   165

Index   177

Research in Labor Problems in the United States

I ____ The Domain of
Labor Problems Research

The subject area of labor problems or labor and industrial relations has won increasing academic recognition in recent decades through the establishment of special university centers or institutes, the development of a number of M.A. and Ph.D. programs, and the publication of several new professional journals. However, it cannot yet be regarded as a discipline like economics or psychology with a generally accepted core of principles, theories, and methods. Rather, it is a *field* of knowledge and study in which all of the traditional social sciences, as well as law and engineering, intersect at different points and in different degrees. Moreover, it is a field with uncertain and shifting boundaries, perceived by students and practitioners from many angles and interests, changing over time, and defying neat definition. As Neil Chamberlain puts it:

Our field sprawls, and the territory we have staked out takes in a polyglot lot of inhabitants with diffuse and often separate interests. Those who inhabit our land range all the way from people with very real and operational problems of an almost how-to-do-it nature, such as at least some who are concerned with personnel administration, to people whose interests are global in scope and abstract in focus, such as at least some of those occupying themselves with the role of labor in economic growth or in the evolutionary process of industrialization. . . . it includes all of those whose interests are touched by labor, whether we think of labor as a functional task, the agent who performs the function, an informal primary society of which he is a part, the formal organizations based on him and his counterparts, a social class, an historical force, a political party, or the subject of governmental regulation.[1]

A recent survey of twelve textbooks used in college introductory labor economics courses revealed not only a tremendous variation in emphasis given to various topics but also the complete omission of certain topics by some authors that other authors regarded as essential.[2] Covered in varying degrees by all of the texts were the history and theories of the labor movement, collective bargaining, the labor force, trade union structure and government, hourly wages, industrial conflict, unemployment, and government regulation. One of the twelve texts made no reference to hours of work; another omitted social security; two left out labor and political action; three ignored the impact of technology on work; and a majority of them were silent on such topics as careers and professions, scientific management, foreign labor experience, labor in economic development, employee organizations other than unions, and types of compensation other than wages.

Had this survey covered branches of the labor field other than economics, such as industrial sociology and industrial psychology, the range of subjects would have been considerably wider, including personnel management, recruitment, training and development, industrial accidents and illness, race relations, immigration, poverty, community organization and power, worker attitudes, leadership and teamwork, and the use of leisure, to cite some of the more important examples.

The scope of a field of knowledge is determined by the research and writing of its scholars. In a field like labor relations, which is so closely tied to contemporary public and private policy formation, the scholars are usually strongly influenced by the issues of their time and the availability of funds to support research on such issues. So-called pure research, based primarily on the intellectual curiosity of the scholar and an interest in knowledge for its own sake, has played a relatively minor role in the labor field. But this does not mean that such research does not result in fundamental knowledge or that it is indifferent to basic theoretical problems. As will be shown, research on labor originated in the intense interests of academicians and public-minded citizens to reform the society of the late nineteenth century and the early twentieth century, subsequently became an instrument of corporate and union as well as public policy-making, and only incidentally (until fairly recent times) became the basis of a scientifically oriented enterprise.

Since the problems of policy-makers may fluctuate widely over short periods of time, it is not surprising that research in the field has also gone through numerous gyrations. A brief review of the post-World War II interval—two decades that may appropriately be called the modern phase in this field—reveals how mobile and diversified contemporary interests have been. In the immediate postwar years, nearly a fifth of the research projects of ten leading university centers[3] were concerned with union-management relations at the plant and industry levels and the causes of industrial peace, reflecting the prevailing national preoccupation with major labor disputes. Next in magnitude of interest was the functioning of the labor market, particularly with respect to the mobility of employees and the role of wages—subjects greatly illuminated by the War Labor Board's experience with wage stabilization and the War Manpower Commission's experience with manpower allocation. The third main area of research was management organization and communication, reflecting on the one hand the resurgence of managerial strength and prestige, after a dismal decade in the 1930's, and on the other hand the delayed impact of the pioneering work of Elton Mayo and his associates, especially the Hawthorne Western Electric study.

By the mid-1950's, two new areas of study were coming to the forefront, although the earlier subjects were still of considerable interest (in fact, there was a tripling of management organization projects). One was the study of labor and industry in other countries, especially in the economically underdeveloped nations, obviously spurred by America's role of world leader. Perhaps the field's most elaborate and expensive project was a four-university investigation of "the labor problem in economic development," financed by the Ford Foundation. The other subject was stimulated by growing public awareness of the economic and psychological difficulties of older workers both prior to and after retirement. A less dramatic increase in research occurred in one of the field's traditional areas, American labor history.

In the first half of the 1960's, new foci of labor research emerged—again attributable in no small measure to public concerns and available funds. The problems of manpower to which attention was directed were very different from those of the 1940's. Interest shifted from the mobility of labor to problems of achieving and maintaining full employment, with a particular emphasis on the characteristics of the unemployed. The unemployed and underemployed Negroes, youth, poorly educated, and unskilled became primary subjects of research—how to educate and train them and how to find new jobs for them. Automation as a source of job displacement as well as of group friction and conflict gained attention. Research interests also turned to investments in human resources as a way of promoting economic growth.

It would be misleading to suggest that all students of labor shifted their research interests with the headlines. Individuals continued to pursue their personal curiosity in diverse segments of the field, often far removed from the contemporary scene. But the mainstream appeared to shift along the channels described above.

The Researchers and Their Institutions

Who are today's researchers in labor problems? Most of them are academicians in the major universities of the country. The bulk of them are economists, usually labeled labor or institutional economists. With the reduced emphasis on institutionalism in the training of economists, many of this group have become or function as industrial relations specialists rather than as economists. A smaller number of the academic researchers are sociologists, psychologists, political scientists, law professors, and engineers.

In the past, they were usually members of the traditional university departments. Thanks to the largess of the Rockefeller family and the Earhart Foundation, six universities—Princeton, Yale, Stanford, Michigan, MIT, and the California Institute of Technology—established special industrial relations sections or bureaus between 1922 and 1938, but their research activities were mainly oriented to the personnel and labor problems of the large corporation.[4] Programs in labor education for unionists also existed in the post-World War I decade at the University of Wisconsin, the University of California at Berkeley, Bryn Mawr, and a few other colleges (as well as at labor-sponsored institutions such as Brookwood Labor College), but research was of only incidental interest to them. Among the Catholic universities with a long interest in labor, Loyola of Chicago was, in 1941, one of the first to set up a teaching-research institute.

Starting in 1944 at Cornell University, there was a sudden movement toward the development of industrial and labor relations centers or institutes to stimulate and conduct teaching and research on a broad interdisciplinary basis. Among the most prominent centers established, in addition to the School of Industrial and Labor Relations at Cornell, were those at California (1945), Chicago (1945), Minnesota (1945), Illinois (1946), and Wisconsin (1947). By 1965, with the addition of the University of Massachusetts, some forty universities in the United States and Canada had joined the procession, although in a few instances older centers had become relatively inactive.

Despite variations in organizational structure and function, almost all of these institutions sponsor faculty and graduate student research. Cornell is the only university that offers the full range of degrees in labor relations from the B.A. to the Ph.D. The specialized master's degree, as distinct from the more customary majors in the several social science departments, is offered at Illinois, Minnesota, Wisconsin, and Michigan State, among others; and the specialized doctorate, with a heavy orientation toward research rather than professional practice, is now available at the first three of these institutions as well as at Cornell.

Research in the field, however, is not limited to the faculties of the centers. Some of the most distinguished contributors come from the social science departments and business schools of universities without formal centers, such as Harvard, Columbia, and Pennsylvania. And there are individuals in other institutions who also devote varying periods of time and varying amounts of resources to labor research. Moreover, in a great many universities, scholars who do not regard themselves as labor relations specialists are conducting research that, directly or indirectly, influences the development of the field. This would apply especially to the general economists interested in the interrelations of national employment, income, productivity, prices, and economic development; to many clinical and social psychologists; to the political scientists analyzing public policy formation; to the sociologists concerned with formal and informal organizations, social roles, social systems and movements, and occupational structure and work; and to certain social and economic historians.

Outside the academic world, research of a significant nature is conducted by branches of the federal government and to a lesser extent by state agencies. It is important, however, to distinguish problem-oriented research from the collection of labor statistics for general and operating purposes and reports on the administration of labor laws. The center of government labor research is the U.S. Department of Labor, notably the Bureau of Labor Statistics but also including, among others, the Office of Manpower Policy, Evaluation, and Research, the Bureau of Employment Security, the Bureau of Apprenticeship and Training, and the Wage and Hour Division. In certain areas, the research of such agencies as the Social Security Administration, the Children's Bureau, the Women's Bureau, and the Office of Education merits reference. Among the states a few labor departments, such as New York, California, and Illinois, occasionally contribute to the development of the field.

The research role of industry and labor has been disappointingly limited. Not more than a score of major industrial firms have produced publishable works of a professional quality relating to labor problems, and even research for internal use is reported to be ignored by many of the leading corporations.[5] The trade unions have been equally delinquent. Many of the larger national or international unions have "research" departments, but these function almost entirely at the service level, compiling simple statistics used in collective bargaining or aiding in the preparation of arbitration and legal briefs. The research department of the American Federation of Labor–Congress of Industrial Organizations, like certain employer-oriented research organizations (e.g., the National Industrial Conference Board and Industrial Relations Counsellors), does a limited amount of original survey work.

It is difficult to estimate the number of persons in the United States who are seriously engaged in labor research at a professionally acceptable level. A first approximation perhaps can be made by ignoring the contributors in marginal categories and confining the estimate to those belonging to the chief association in the field, the Industrial Relations Research Association (not all of whose members do research), or contributing to the major journals—*Industrial and Labor Relations Review, Industrial Relations, Labor History,* and the *Monthly Labor Review.* This total would probably range between 600 and 800. To it might be added a few hundred others in labor organizations, industry, government, and the universities who are not IRRA members.

Contemporary Attitudes and Problems

In the nineteen annual meetings since its founding in 1948, the IRRA has devoted eleven specific sessions to the challenges and dilemmas of labor research, and six of the presidential addresses have been directed to the same general topic. An examination of these papers reveals an interesting variety of views among the leading scholars of the field as to the role and status of research. Several important issues emerge for none of which a simple answer exists: Is industrial relations an art or science? Should research be theory oriented or confined to description and classification? In selecting topics for research, should contemporary policy be given top priority? Are interdisciplinary approaches to the major problems of the field feasible and desirable? To what extent should reliance be placed on team research as opposed to the study of individual scholars? Are the universities so dependent on institutional ties with governmental, management, and labor organizations as to discourage research challenging the status quo? What are the appropriate relations between the university scholars and the governmental agencies in the field?

Each of these questions, which will be treated more fully in subsequent chapters, from a historical as well as a contemporary view, warrants brief comment here.

Art or Science?

One of the more cogent statements on this question was made by J. Douglas Brown in his IRRA presidential address of December 28, 1952:

Industrial relations, like all other sub-divisions of what we call social science, is truly a branch of the humanities. Social science uses the proper sciences more as a *tool* than as a *determinant*. Industrial Relations is the study of a humane art with the use, where relevant, of scientific methodology. Industrial Relations is not a science. Rather it is the study of the values arising in the minds, intuitions, and emotions of individuals as these values become embodied in group organization and action. The understanding and solution of problems of group organization and action can never be divorced from the more basic understanding of the values which determine individual behavior. No matter how useful scientific methodology may be along the way, the goal of industrial relations research and practice lies beyond the "timber line" of science.[6]

It is difficult to quarrel with Dean Brown's emphasis on the importance of human values in industrial relations, but the implication that human values do not lend themselves to scientific inquiry in the fullest meaning of that concept is highly debatable. The nub of the problem is the meaning of scientific inquiry. If the phrase means the search for generalizations about selected variables and factors through the formulation of key questions and hypotheses that are subjected to empirical verification or refutation, then behavior and values relating to it in the labor field are no more exempt from scientific inquiry than any other type of behavior, whether human or not. Admittedly, the search for generalization in the behavioral and social sciences is more complex and has been far less successful than that in the area of the physical sciences. The objectives and approaches of such a search are, however, no less valid.

Whether the study of labor is regarded as an art or science is important because of its possible consequences. The artist is primarily concerned with the uniqueness of things; he studies a variety of cases for insights and illustrations rather than general rules; subjective "truth" or "integrity" is his ultimate test. The scientist, in contrast, is mainly concerned with the general; he studies a variety of cases for commonalities and differences; objectivity is his goal and criterion. It would, of course, be absurd to draw a rigid line between art and science. Each embodies ingredients of the other.

Theory and Research

A related issue is whether research should be theory oriented or whether the field is too underdeveloped to warrant going beyond the stages of description and classification. Both sides of the issue have been raised by scholars at Harvard University. Sumner Slichter, James Healy, and E. Robert Livernash, in the introduction to their major study of the impact of collective bargaining on management, have written:

The authors do not believe that the time is ripe to push very far with theories of the determinants of industrial relations . . . The factors involved in industrial relations are so numerous and occur in so many combinations and permutations that worthwhile theories are difficult to formulate.

What is important is to know what is going on and to
see that every industrial relations situation is more or less
unique and must be explained as a whole.[7]

Their colleague, John Dunlop, in a seminal work
of theoretical character, has taken the opposite position:

While there is no disposition here to deprecate the gathering
of facts of industrial relations, and many additional detailed
studies are imperative, the field of industrial relations today
may be described in the words of Julian Huxley: "Moun-
tains of facts have been piled up on the plains of human
ignorance. . . . The result is a glut of raw material. Great
piles of facts are lying around unutilized, or utilized only
in an occasional and partial manner." Facts have outrun
ideas. Integrating theory has lagged far behind expanding
experience. The many worlds of industrial relations have
been changing more rapidly than the ideas to interpret, to
explain, and to relate them.[8]

From what has gone before, it is clear that this author
strongly endorses the Dunlop view.

Should Labor Research Be Mainly
Policy Oriented?

Most scholars in the field have tended to give an
affirmative answer to the question of whether or not
labor research should be policy oriented. Such an
attitude is consistent with the highly pragmatic character of much of American social science. It gives a
field a sense of vitality and immediacy that is highly
rewarding to its practitioners. But it has dangers as
well as benefits. The main danger arises from the fact
that the problems facing the policy-makers, whether
in government, industry, or the unions, change so
rapidly in this dynamic society that there is often

simply not enough time to do the careful type of research that can be helpful to policy formation or to accumulate the basic knowledge on which scientific principles can be erected. The history of scientific development in the physical and natural sciences suggests that a vast amount of study of underlying theoretical principles, as well as descriptive factual evidence, is necessary before meaningful scientific contributions to practice can be made. The students of labor, and even more their clients in government and industry, appear not to have fully absorbed this lesson. The exciting problems of the moment as well as the availability of research funds seem to have dictated the course of research. As a result, a number of research undertakings have achieved a passing notice, but few have contributed appreciably to either policy-making or to the development of a scientific body of knowledge.

Once again one must avoid overstating a point. Empirical knowledge has accumulated over the years in many segments of the field and has proved useful and timely to policy-makers. Examples are the wage and price studies carried out by the Bureau of Labor Statistics for the War Labor Board, the labor market analyses used in the antipoverty program, and the job satisfaction and employee attitude survey data utilized in company communication programs.

Interdisciplinary Approaches

Until World War II, most of the research in labor was performed by institutional economists who recognized that the traditional tools of economists by themselves were inadequate to cope with many of the major problems of the field. Thus the institutionalists borrowed freely from other disciplines and created their own interdisciplinary concepts. As the several social sciences refined their disciplines, however, they began to produce labor relations specialists of their own, with more highly developed tools than those of the institutionalists in particular areas. Thus in the post-World War II period, the new institutes and centers were largely constructed on a multidisciplinary basis, and a significant number of interdisciplinary research projects were undertaken.

The relative merits of the interdisciplinary approach are still being debated. Its proponents note that only through the utilization of the concepts and techniques of several disciplines can labor problems properly be studied and analyzed. By combining the disciplines as dictated by the problems, the research will have the benefit of the most advanced and sophisticated developments in these disciplines. The opponents of interdisciplinary research argue that this approach is unduly time-consuming and that it forces compromises which involve a watering-down of disciplinary standards.

Both sets of arguments have merit and, therefore, lead to a third approach—namely, research by students trained in more than one discipline. Such is the aim of the new graduate programs (at both the M.A. and Ph.D. levels) in industrial relations as distinct from the traditional programs in labor economics, industrial psychology, etc. These new programs do not contemplate the replacement of the disciplinary programs—the more narrowly trained specialist still has an important place in research, both as to unidisciplinary problems (such as the impact on the volume of employment of a steel price rise) and as to consultation on multidisciplinary problems (such as the implications of rapid technological change in the newspaper industry). The more broadly trained researcher would not only be better equipped to work with the specialist but also would be able to carry on separate research into many of the field's problems.

Individual Versus Team Research?

This question is partly related to the preceding, but it also applies to the team of similarly trained students. In the physical and biological sciences, team research has been widely accepted and productive. It may be true, as is often asserted, that great ideas come only from individuals, but it is also true that individuals learn from one another and that in empirical work the individual, even with a number of junior aides, is extremely limited in the scope of his research. In many aspects of labor research, the need for teamwork has particular justification because so much of the primary data can be obtained only by interviewing and observation in the field—a highly expensive and time-consuming process.

On the other hand, individual research continues to merit support as well. There are still many problems, especially of a documentary nature, that can profitably be studied on a small-scale basis. Even in the case of larger problems, the individual can often perform exploratory work leading to the development of useful hypotheses and questions. And the replication of large studies on a smaller scale can often be a fruitful way of testing earlier findings.

Challenging Prevailing Values

In a celebrated series of lectures in 1938,[9] Robert S. Lynd indicted contemporary social research for being so culture-bound as to be incapable of seriously exploring and challenging the prevailing values and institutions of society. This indictment has particular relevance to the industrial relations field because the institutions with which it deals—labor unions, corporations, and political parties—are among the most powerful in the nation, and conflicts and competition among them make objective research exceedingly difficult. Notwithstanding the great tradition of academic freedom, professors do not lightly undertake to attack or seriously question either the premises on which the institutions operate or the manner in which they carry out their functions. For one thing, serious field research usually requires the extensive cooperation of organizations and their leaders, and this cooperation will not be forthcoming if there is an expectation that the findings may be unfavorable to them. To take sides in a controversy may close important doors to the researcher in the future. Another factor is to be found in the general climate of the country since World War II, which has been unfavorable to "radical" thought, tending to place it in a "cold war" framework even though it may not have the slightest connection with Communist ideology. Research of a Marxist orientation is particularly discouraged; in contrast to British, European, and Japanese output, the American research literature has been oriented almost entirely within a capitalistic or moderate welfare state framework.

No science, of course, can progress if it is content to accept the status quo or the values of powerful leaders. Since the scientific approach is problem directed, its practitioners must feel free to question widely and to pursue their questioning wherever the analysis and facts lead them, making due allowance for their own value systems. Otherwise, the researchers become technicians content to accept the values of others and not genuine searchers for the truth.

Relations Between University and Government

The U.S. Bureau of Labor Statistics, with more than 700 professional employees, is probably the largest compiler of labor data in the world. If to its voluminous collections are added the data gathered by other branches of the Department of Labor in addition to other federal agencies, the supply of government-produced data appears enormous. In comparison with this output, the numbers of persons involved, the monies expended, the data output, and the resources of the universities seem relatively small.

In general, however, the government agencies have pursued the more cautious but far from trivial role of data collector and summarizer rather than of data analyst and theorist. The university scholars, on the other hand, have not hesitated to search for connections among variables and generalizations of both a descriptive and causal character, even on the basis of extremely limited evidence.

This difference in approach is one of degree and should not be exaggerated. Government agencies have made important contributions through their research, especially in the field of labor statistics. Nonetheless, the development of the field has been handicapped because a wealth of data (especially the unpublished) has remained unused, even unknown. In recent years, the flaws in this situation have been noted,[10] and increased efforts to integrate data gathering with analysis have been made. The Labor Department has permitted more interpretative report writing by its

most competent personnel and has given leaves of
absence to some of them at universities for thinking
and writing in the field; it has also contracted with
university scholars to conduct studies and to exploit
available data. Promise of more extensive developments of this type was contained in the initial statement of the new Commissioner of Labor Statistics,
Arthur M. Ross, on taking office in October, 1965:

I propose that we put greater emphasis on cogent analysis
and interpretation as well as fact-gathering and reporting.
As Ewan Clague (the retiring Commissioner) has noted so
frequently in his speeches and writings, the purpose of
economic data is to provide a rational basis for decision
making and policy formulation. The BLS does not and
should not formulate policies, but it can and should present
impartial, competent analysis of the data in terms which are
relevant to the policy issues.[11]

This point of view, one strongly supported by the
Secretary of Labor, W. Willard Wirtz, will be examined more fully in the final chapter of this volume.

Origins
in Reformism

The beginnings of labor research in the United States may be traced to the legislative investigations of Massachusetts into child labor in the 1820's and into the hours of female textile workers in the 1830's and 1840's; but sustained and systematic study of labor problems began only after the establishment of the state bureaus of labor, the first of which was in Massachusetts in 1869. Within the next fifteen years, eleven other states followed suit, and in 1884 Congress established a Bureau of Labor in the Department of the Interior, which was subsequently to evolve into the present Department of Labor. These bureaus were the product of agitation by labor leaders and middle-class reformers for statistics and other factual data to support their legislative and economic demands, as well as the desire to have a governmental agency that would reflect the interests of labor. An outstanding figure in this drive was William Sylvis, president of the then powerful Iron Molders Union and of the National Labor Union, one of the main predecessors of the American Federation of Labor. Sylvis was impressed by the role of the labor department in Prussia

and introduced what is believed to be the first resolution for such a department to be adopted by an
American labor organization at the 1868 convention
of the National Labor Union.[1]

The man who was preeminently responsible for the
shaping of the research of the bureaus, however, was
Carroll D. Wright, the father of labor statistics in the
United States. A lawyer by training, and a frustrated
politician, Wright moved into the field of labor
statistics quite accidently and did not appreciate its
possible contribution to social reform until he had
served two terms as Commissioner of Labor Statistics
in Massachusetts and directed a number of population
and industrial censuses in the state. By making the
Massachusetts bureau a model for the country, Wright
became a natural choice for appointment as the first
U.S. Commissioner of Labor in 1885, a post he held
for twenty years.[2]

As James Leiby points out, the investigations of the
bureaus focused originally on specific problems and
only later, in the early years of the twentieth century,
turned to the accumulation of trend data or statistical
series.[3] Among the topics covered in the annual reports of the Massachusetts bureau between 1874 and
1886 were: education and employment of young persons and children; the sanitary condition of working
people in their homes and employments; comparative
rates of wages and hours of labor in Massachusetts
and foreign countries; the prices of provisions, clothing, rent, etc., in Massachusetts and Europe; cooperation; industrial arbitration and conciliation in
England and Massachusetts; pauperism and crime;
conjugal condition, nativities, and ages of married
women and mothers; the unemployed; convict labor;
hours of labor; drunkenness and liquor selling; citi-

zenship; wages, prices, and profits; employers' liability
for personal injuries to their employees; Sunday labor;
and art in industry.

Similarly, the annual and special reports of the
Federal Bureau of Labor between 1886 and 1905
covered: industrial depressions; convict labor; strikes
and lockouts; working women in large cities; railroad
labor; cost of production; industrial education; building and loan associations; wages and hours; cost of
living and retail prices of food; marriage and divorce;
labor laws; compulsory insurance in Germany; the
Gothenburg system of liquor traffic; the slums of Chicago and other cities; the housing of working people;
regulation and restriction of output; and coal mine
labor in Europe.

Methodologically, these studies had many limitations and imperfections, but this is hardly surprising in
view of the then undeveloped state of statistical theory
(such as sampling and index numbers) and the limited
funds appropriated for the operations of the bureaus.
Nonetheless, they provided a mass of information that
contributed significantly to the enactment of state and
federal labor laws and that are indispensable to an
understanding of the history of labor in the United
States. Indeed, much of the data on the nineteenth century have not been adequately exploited by labor historians to this day.

One of the first of the academicians to take advantage of the reports of the bureaus and to make the
study of labor problems a major preoccupation was
Richard T. Ely of Johns Hopkins University (1881–
1892) and the University of Wisconsin (1892 until
about 1904, when he brought in John R. Commons to
assume leadership in the labor field, while Ely himself
turned to other economic themes). During his Hopkins

period, Ely was one of the leaders of the new economists who rejected the deductive theorizing of the
older economists, called for historical and statistical
research into the problems of the day, and demolished
the premise that economic problems, such as labor
problems, were governed by the laws of laissez-faire
economics and could not be remedied by the action
of the state. Ely was a key leader in the formation,
in 1885, of the American Economic Association on
a platform proclaiming that "We regard the State as
an agency whose positive assistance is one of the
indispensable conditions of human progress."[4] He
was then a Christian Socialist, and his pioneering
volume, *The Labor Movement in America,* had a
highly reformist flavor.

This reformist approach is explicitly displayed in
the preface to the study. Ely stated that one of the
two chief purposes of the volume (which he hoped
would ultimately become a History of Labor in the
New World) was "to convince my readers of the
vastness of our present opportunities. . . . It is still
in our power permanently to avoid many of the evils
under which older countries suffer, if we will but
take to heart the lessons of past experience, and seriously endeavor to profit by the mistakes of others."[5]
Ely went on to note "the wilful falsehood with which
one's character and motives are assailed, when one
attempts to treat social topics truthfully," and he felt
constrained to stress that this was "a most conservative
work." In a special section addressed "to workingmen,"
he urged them to improve their effort and character; to
abstain from drink—the poor man's curse and the
rich man's shame; to beware of political partyism;
to avoid violence and stay within the law; to cast aside
envy and admire genuine superiority; to educate,

organize, and wait; and to have faith in Christ and the support of the ministry.

In contrast to the governmental studies, Ely's labor writings were primarily historical and interpretative rather than statistical and descriptive. He was particularly interested in the institutions of labor, in the way they had evolved over time and in the structures, procedures, and policies they had developed. In *An Introduction to Political Economy,* which appeared three years after *The Labor Movement in America,* he gave considerable emphasis to the evolution of economic society and included a major section on wages, labor organizations, profit sharing, cooperation, and socialism. In this volume, we find what appears to be one of the first conscious efforts to conceptualize and define "industrial democracy."[6] He assiduously gathered books, pamphlets, and newspapers as well as constitutions, bylaws, and annual proceedings of labor organizations, and he appealed to his readers to send him whatever such materials they possessed, particularly earlier publications and oral or written communications relating to them. In 1904, at Wisconsin, he established the American Bureau of Industrial Research "for the purpose of preparing a full and complete history of American industrial society."

Ely's writings are no longer studied except by historians, but his influence on the study of labor was enormous because of the work of his students at Johns Hopkins and Wisconsin. For several decades, these students were leaders in academic circles concerned with the field.

Ely's graduate student, John R. Commons, emulated him in his concern for using social and economic research to bring about a more just society. Because of his zeal in raising challenging questions

and pursuing primary data, Commons often ran
counter to the conservative attitudes of his university
administrators, and although he was in no sense a
radical, he was obliged to leave teaching posts at Indiana and Syracuse Universities, and for five years,
until receiving Ely's invitation to Wisconsin, he was
unable to obtain an academic position. He put these
five years to good advantage, however, helping to
organize a private bureau of economic research, serving as investigator for the U.S. Industrial Commission,
collaborating on an economic yearbook, and acting as
conciliator, secretary, and statistician for the National
Civic Federation.

Commons went to Wisconsin to work on Ely's
projected history of industrial democracy in the United
States. By 1910–1911, he and his students had completed the famous eleven-volume *Documentary History
of Industrial Society,* out of which came the two-
volume *History of Labor in the United States,* still
the standard work on labor in the nineteenth century.
But history was only one of his research interests. During his three decades of teaching and study at Wisconsin, Commons revealed an extraordinary versatility
in his approach to the scholar's role, and reference to
his work will necessarily be made in the two succeeding
chapters as well as in this one. His views about labor
research were expressed in an address entitled "Constructive Research" before the New York School of
Philanthropy in September, 1907.[7]

Commons divided research into three categories—
academic, agitational, and constructive. Academic
research is fundamental and "must always have the
first place" because it is "truth for its own sake," the
pioneering development of the principles of a science.
Agitational research "awakens the public"; it "carries

conviction that something must be done." It has the function of exposure, of locating social disease, of muckraking, and has been left to the journalists because of academic precautions. The curing or preventing of social ills is the work of constructive research. It is "the sort of inquiry that goes along with administration and is designed to improve it." Constructive research for Commons "gives exact information for the public to work upon. . . . It reduces the coercive functions of government and increases the part played by persuasion." Commons saw in his historical study the equivalence to the laboratory experiment as a way of conducting constructive research.

Commons' reformist inclinations were realistic, not utopian, as he clearly indicated in a short essay about the University of Wisconsin's educational approach, which he labeled Utilitarian Idealism.[8] The modern problem, he stated in 1909, was how to combine idealism and utilitarianism in the same persons or, in other terms, leisure and work. This meant shorter hours of work at reasonable pay and more opportunity for education. The purpose of education was to develop the ethical ideal of work—service to others. A half dozen years later, in 1915, while serving as a member of the U.S. Commission on Industrial Relations, Commons displayed his utilitarian idealism in a minority report:

Before recommending any additional, much needed laws affecting wages, hours, child and woman labor, unemployment, or other substantive laws to improve industrial conditions, we must call attention to the widespread breakdown of existing laws and must devise methods of revising them and enacting and enforcing new laws so that they will fit actual conditions and be enforceable and enforced. With the widespread demand for more laws to remedy widespread and well recognized causes of industrial unrest, there is a curious feeling that, if only more laws are placed on the statute books, they will, in some unexplained way, get themselves enforced. While recognizing the justice of much of this demand for new laws, we are not placing them first in our report but rather the methods of investigating conditions, of enacting legislation, of judicial interpretation and administrative enforcement necessary to make them worthwhile as a real remedy.[9]

Although permeated with reformist values, the research of academicians like Ely and Commons was not "agitational" in character. During the two decades before American involvement in World War I, however, there was an important body of researchers whose main objective was to expose the social ills of the country, particularly as they related to working people. These researchers were mainly social workers, journalists, or well-to-do, socialistically minded reformers who gave much of the coloration to the progressive movement. They were individuals whose consciences had been shocked by the abuses of a booming, immensely profitable, largely unrestrained capitalism, with its great corporations and trusts, its striking disparities in income, its teeming urban slums and ghettos, and its fierce industrial conflicts. Among the pioneers were the Hull House group in Chicago, under the dynamic leadership of Jane Addams. One of the "residents" of Hull House was Florence Kelley, later the first factory inspector in Illinois, who suggested and then carried out for the Illinois State Bureau of Labor a study of the sweating system and child labor in Chicago.

The center of this movement, however, was in New York City and particularly in the group that sponsored and contributed to *The Survey,* for many years a

weekly publication of the Charity Organization Society
of the City of New York. The name of its publisher
was misleading because *The Survey* (which until 1909
was called *Charities and the Commons*) was designed
"to spread the news of social advance and to recruit
workers in behalf of the common welfare."[10] *The
Survey* group contained most of the prominent
"moderate" social reformers of the period, including
academicians like Edward T. Devine (one of its
editors), Commons, Simon Patten, and Samuel
McCune Lindsay; its national influence was reflected
in the appointment of the Commission on Industrial
Relations upon its petition to President Taft following
the Los Angeles *Times* explosion case in 1910 that
rocked the country.

One of the prominent figures in *The Survey* group
was Paul Kellogg, who directed the Pittsburgh Survey
of 1907 and 1908 for the Russell Sage Foundation.
The Pittsburgh study was originally undertaken by the
then *Charities and the Commons* for a special number
of the magazine. The foundation, which was just
getting started, decided to enlarge and deepen its
scope on a scale comparable to the famous Booth
study of the London poor. The six volumes that followed set the pattern for numerous community social
studies in the United States. In his introduction to one
of the volumes, *The Steel Workers,* by John A. Fitch,
Kellogg revealed something of the spirit that underlay
the research. Noting that the largest employer of
steel workers in Pittsburgh was also the largest employer of labor in America at the time, he said:

So far as the mills and the shifts that man them go, the
steel operators possess what many another manager and
industrial president has hankered after and has been denied
—untrammeled control. What has this exceptional em-

ployer done with this exceptional control over the human forces of production? Here our findings state concretely the problems of an industrial democracy in ways which cannot be lightly thrust aside.

. . .

Underlying the initial reasons for such a portrayal of labor conditions in the steel industry is another reason which developed in the course of the inquiry, and which, as with the Mariner's tale, leaves no choice open as to the telling. The issues which Mr. Fitch takes up are of a sort which are not publicly discussed in the mill towns of the Pittsburgh district. Old employees do not dare petition their employers to consider them. Men have been discharged for calling meetings to discuss them. It would mean instant dismissal for large numbers of men should they act together to effect these things in the way that farmers would take up freight rates or the price of apples at a grange hall; and dismissal would mean the entire dislocation of life. . . . It is fully time to bring these issues out into the open, where a man will not risk his livelihood by discussing it. That is the manner of America.[11]

Another active *The Survey* figure was John B. Andrews, long-time secretary of the American Association for Labor Legislation. The association, as one of its members observed, had as its main purpose "action, not talk; hence its publications are practical rather than academic."[12] Nevertheless, the research stimulated by the association was of a high professional order and compared favorably with the best in the field. The precedent-setting Brandeis brief of 1907 in the case of *Muller vs. Oregon* (pertaining to the constitutionality of the Oregon ten-hour law for women) was one example. The research by William M. Leiserson on unemployment for the New York State Commission on Employers' Liability was another. Many of Commons' students and associates at Wisconsin, including Edwin E. Witte, David J. Saposs, Don Lescohier, and John Fitch were important contributors. Such work laid the basis for the highly influential *Principles of Labor Legislation* by Commons and Andrews, first published in 1916, which went through four editions, the last in 1936.

Somewhat to the left of *The Survey* group (with overlapping) was the Intercollegiate Socialist Society, which was formed in 1905 by Upton Sinclair and Jack London, among others, and which became the League for Industrial Democracy in 1921. Adherents of the society, like Sinclair, W. J. Ghent, and Robert Hunter, were significant participants in the war on poverty and social injustice of the Progressive period.[13]

The reformist impulse was also an important ingredient in the research performed by the staffs of both the Industrial Commission of 1898–1902 and the Commission on Industrial Relations of 1913–1915. In the case of the former, the central concern seemed to be the dramatic rise and attendant abuses of the industrial and financial trusts, although the commission was authorized to and did investigate numerous other problems, including those of labor. The list of labor problems indeed covered the entire gamut from the general conditions of employment and unemployment, wages and hours, and technology through a comprehensive industry-by-industry examination of labor organizations, working conditions, collective bargaining, and strikes. Labor legislation, the bureaus of labor statistics, factory inspection, child labor, the employment of women, accidents and compensation, convict labor, free employment agencies, labor on public works, cooperation and profit sharing, industrial training and education, immigration, labor in

the south, two serious strikes in Chicago, and procedures for the settlement of labor disputes—all drew
the commission's attention.

The Commission on Industrial Relations concentrated its attention on labor problems in what was the
most elaborate governmental inquiry in the history
of the field. Ironically, because of internal dissensions
and a three-way report, as well as the distraction of
public interest from its work due to the outbreak of
World War I, the commission had little direct impact
on federal legislation. It provided, however, a highly
valuable opportunity for research to a staff recruited
mainly from the universities and that included such
outstanding contemporary and future leaders in the
field as George E. Barnett, Robert F. Hoxie, Selig
Perlman, William M. Leiserson, W. Jett Lauck, Sumner Slichter, Leo Wolman, David A. McCabe, and
Edwin E. Witte. The staff was used not only to lay
the groundwork for the extensive public hearings
that were held throughout the country and to analyze
the data presented, but also to make special investigations on specific problem areas. The reports by
Hoxie on scientific management and labor, by Barnett
and McCabe on mediation and arbitration, by Wolman on the extent and growth of labor organizations,
and by Witte on injunctions in labor disputes, to cite
only a few, became the basis for standard works in
the literature on labor.

The reformist spirit which dominated the work of
the commission and its staff was reflected in both
The Survey group's petition leading to the establishment of the commission and in the report prepared
by Basil M. Manly, Director of Research and Investigation for the commission, which was signed by the
chairman, Frank P. Walsh, and the three labor members.

The petition, after reciting the broad social and industrial issues raised by the confession and conviction of the McNamara brothers in the Los Angeles *Times* explosion case, concluded with the following recommendation to President Taft:

Today, as fifty years ago, a house divided against itself cannot stand. We have yet to solve the problems of democracy in its industrial relationships and to solve them along democratic lines. On the same vitality, the same idealism, the same constructive justice of the people which stood the stress of Lincoln's time, we ground our confidence in petitioning the President and the Congress of the United States to appoint a commission to investigate, study, and consider the grave problems of internal statesmanship herein set forth.[14]

Similarly, the Manly report began with the declaration:

The question of industrial relations assigned by Congress to the Commission for investigation is more fundamental and of greater importance to the welfare of the Nation than any other question except the form of our Government. The only hope for the solution of the tremendous problems created by industrial relationship [sic] lies in the effective use of our democratic institutions and in the rapid extension of the principles of democracy to industry.[15]

During and for a few years after World War I, labor research was strongly influenced by another reformist theme which became popularly known as "industrial democracy." This term acquired a variety of meanings.[16] For the dominant faction in the labor movement led by Samuel Gompers, it was almost synonymous with trade unionism and collective bargaining. For the most radical elements in the labor movement, it meant the elimination of the capitalist wage system and its replacement by a socialist system

controlled by the workers. For some of the less extreme reformers, it meant public ownership of particular industries with tripartite administration by
representatives of management, labor, and the public:
a leading example derived from government operation
of the railroads during the war was the Plumb Plan
for the railroad and mining industries. For some of
the early management exponents of employee representation plans, such as the Filenes, John Leitch, and
John D. Rockefeller, Jr., it meant committee systems
for workers without unions. For still others, it meant
profit sharing, industrial copartnership, or producers'
cooperatives. Whatever its meaning, industrial democracy became the subject of innumerable writings,
including some of a high-level research caliber.

Since the early 1920's, reformism has played a relatively less important role in labor research, but it has
continued to be a strong motivating factor to the
present day. In the twenties and early thirties, it was
reflected particularly in studies of the need for protective labor legislation, especially for children and
women, but also to counter unemployment and the
privations of old age. Less conspicuously, it generated
a number of studies in union structure, mainly by those
who believed that craft unionism was causing the
stagnation of the labor movement and that industrial
unionism was the chief solution. During the New Deal
years, there was much of the crusading spirit of the
prewar decade in the area of union organization, as
well as in that of social security. The activities of the
Senate subcommittee headed by Robert La Follette,
Jr., of Wisconsin, in the areas of free speech, labor
rights, industrial espionage, company unions, and industrial violence were less comprehensive than the
work of the Commission on Industrial Relations, but

their impact on public opinion and federal and state legislation was much greater.

Since World War II, two other aspects of labor research have had a reformist flavor. One of these was primarily a phenomenon of the 1950's and concerned the internal operations of the now powerful trade unions. Investigations by the Senate's McClellan Committee into the affairs of the Teamsters and a few other unions aroused widespread public interest, stimulated considerable journalistic and some academic research, and led to the passage of the Landrum-Griffin Act in 1959, regulating the internal affairs of unions. Concurrently, the inquiry sponsored by The Fund for the Republic[17] into the relationship between the large organization (especially unions and corporations) and the individual member also reflected a growing anxiety over the dehumanizing position of the individual in a mass technological society.

Another labor problem that appealed to reformist instincts emerged in the 1960's. Even more than the first, it paralleled a major trend of the pre-World War I period—the concern with the problem of poverty. The two contexts were, of course, very different. In the earlier period, poverty was attached largely to the new immigrants who, because of differences in language and culture, had not yet been assimilated into American life. The movement out of poverty, if not for the first generation immigrant, then for his children, was expected to be accomplished through hard work, initiative, and education. The government's role was viewed chiefly in negative terms, that is, to prevent exploitation of the weak by the strong. In the later period, the problem of poverty had strong racial overtones and was seen, in considerable measure, as a function of discrimination. Moreover, the government's role was not merely that of eliminating discrimination through legislation, but also of providing education and training for work in the new technological society and of providing jobs to the extent that the private economy was unable to do so. In both periods, journalists helped to promote public interest in the problem, while academicians provided the essential studies in depth.

Research as an Instrument of Administration

The line between reformist research and research as an instrument of administration is not always easy to draw. Arbitrarily, under the administrative category, one may include research performed for an organization (government, business, or union) to enable it to operate more effectively. In contrast, reformist research may be defined as that which is intended to bring to light the need for drastic alterations in existing practice or thinking, or to establish a new program for remedying social ills.

Research for Government

One of the outstanding early examples of research for more effective administration is the work by Commons and his students in the state government of Wisconsin during the regime of the Progressive Republicans led by Robert La Follette.[1] This Wisconsin relationship between state government and state university did not start with Commons or focus only on labor matters, but the labor aspect was a significant one. In 1905, Commons was asked by the then Governor Robert La Follette to draft a Civil Service law, and two years later, after La Follette had become Senator, Commons drafted the state Public Utility Act at his suggestion. Together with Charles McCarthy of the Wisconsin Legislative Reference Library, Commons made the drafting of proposed laws a function of experts based on extensive research. In 1911, a similar cooperative effort led to the adoption of a law establishing the Wisconsin Industrial Commission on which Commons served for two years. The commission was given responsibility for administration of all Wisconsin labor legislation, of which the most important applied to workmen's compensation and industrial safety. Very much later, in 1932, during the gubernatorial term of Philip La Follette, the same process led to the enactment of unemployment insurance, also to be administered by the industrial commission. Commons and his students did much of its drafting, research, and implementation.

Commons' philosophy of research in government was brilliantly depicted in the report that he wrote as a member of the United States Commission on Industrial Relations in 1915. In this report, he strongly advocated the adoption, on both the state and federal levels, of Wisconsin-type industrial commissions to administer labor laws, using tripartite advisory councils (of employer, employee, and public representatives) as critics and consultants. Under the heading of "investigations" he wrote:

These recommendations regarding investigations are the most important of all the recommendations regarding the Industrial Commission. . . . Investigations furnish the basis for drafting laws by the legislature, for formulating rules and regulations by the Commission, for interpretation of laws and rules by the courts, and for prosecutions in enforcing the laws. . . . All labor legislation, all administration of labor laws, all efforts at mediation and arbitration, all recommendations of public bodies, go back, for their justification, to statistics and investigations. The money of the Government is worse than wasted and the officials are discredited if there remains any interested body of citizens who do not place confidence in these official statistics and investigations.[2]

Research as an instrument of federal government policy-making and administration was increasingly practiced after 1915. Examples may be cited from three important periods—World War I, the New Deal, and World War II. In the first of these periods, an interesting case is the research done for the Eight-Hour Commission appointed by President Wilson in accordance with the 1916 act establishing the eight-hour standard workday for railroad employees. The act provided that a commission be appointed to "observe the operation and effects of the institution of the eight-hour standard workday as above defined and the facts and conditions affecting the relations between such common carriers and employees during a period of not less than six months nor more than nine months, in the discretion of the commission, and within thirty days thereafter such commission shall report its findings to the President and Congress."[3] The commission employed three well-known specialists, William Z. Ripley, Victor S. Clark, and Charles P. Howard, to carry out the required inquiries, and although the work was hampered by wartime conditions, the detailed reports were impressive research products—even as judged by contemporary standards.

This type of scholarly evaluative research has been uncommon, and it is interesting to note that at a conference of prominent industrial relations scholars sponsored by the General Electric Company in 1965, research evaluating the consequences of legislative and private policy-making was given the highest priority.

The Eight-Hour Commission's report, despite its high quality, did not lead to any significant change in policy or procedures. Another commission had a more important impact on the railroad industry. Shortly after the government took over operation of the industry in December, 1917, Director General William G. McAdoo was confronted with serious labor unrest regarding wages and working conditions. He therefore appointed a top-level commission to investigate "the compensation of persons in the railroad service, the relation of railroad wages to wages in other industries, the conditions respecting wages in different parts of the country," as well as the special emergency arising from the war. The commission not only made an exhaustive study of American conditions but also studied the experiences of Great Britain and France. Many of the recommendations of this study were embodied in a general order of the Director General regulating wages and conditions during the war.[4]

The Department of Labor used research in a variety of ways to contribute to the government's administration of the wartime labor program. Its Information and Education Service sent a group of representative employers to Europe to investigate employer attitudes toward labor problems, the attitudes of labor leaders and workers, and the policies of governments to allay labor unrest. Among the subjects surveyed were the shop-steward movement, the Whitley plan, unemployment insurance, health insurance, wages, hours, hous-

ing, and compulsory arbitration. This type of research
was bound to be superficial and impressionistic, but
it apparently influenced the thinking of government
administrators as well as of the general public. A
Training and Dilution Section was also established
by the Labor Department that included among its
functions "to ascertain the best methods used in industrial establishments for training workers to do
specific kinds of work; to discover the need for such
training; to provide information on this subject to
industrial managers and employees; to inspect the
operation of training schemes and make a report con-
cerning them." According to Gordon Watkins, the
experience of this section taught the nation that any
system of industrial training must include a clearing-
house of methods and experience, a staff of well-trained
experts to study and analyze the special problems of
particular industries, and channels for the dissemi-
nation of knowledge.[5] Other agencies of the Labor Department that utilized research procedures, especially
for the war program, included a Working Conditions
Service and a Commission on Living Conditions.

During the New Deal period, academicians in unprecedented numbers joined governmental agencies,
and their training and outlook, as well as the neces-
sities of the time, contributed to a substantial expansion of research as an instrument of policy-making
and administration. The National Industrial Recovery
Act codes of fair competition were a major early example. In order to make sure that the codes submitted by trade associations or by joint employer-
union groups met the standards of the act with respect
to minimum wages, maximum hours, child labor, labor
organization, and other provisions, the NRA staff
was obliged to compile considerable information about

each industry. Moreover, in many industries, neither employer nor labor organizations were available to draw up satisfactory codes, and the NRA itself drew up the code.

A somewhat similar type of research was done by a unit of the National Labor Relations Board. Under the direction of one of Commons' earliest and most able assistants, David J. Saposs, the board's research unit made numerous studies of the extent to which manufacturing and other industries in interstate commerce provided support for the constitutionality of the Wagner Act, as well as providing a basis for determining jurisdictional questions in cases coming to the board. Other studies dealt with the subjects of appropriate bargaining units, the results of the disestablishment of company unions, collective bargaining agreements, election results, compliance with board orders, and various unfair labor practices. In 1940, pressure from the Congress led to the elimination of the research unit for reasons which were politically inspired, and this highly valuable type of administrative research was, thereafter, sharply curtailed.

Other New Deal agencies in the labor field, such as the Social Security Administration and the Wage and Hour and Public Contracts Division, also found it essential to set up research units. Such units were established not only to compile statistics and other facts of a reporting nature but also to conduct studies that would aid the administrators in the execution of their programs, including the determining of policies, the making of minimum wage decisions, and the formulation of proposals for improvement.

These developments were further elaborated during World War II in the experience of the National War Labor Board. Research in the NWLB had a dual role.

On the one hand, the wage analysis division found that traditional knowledge about wage structures, both within the individual firm and in a labor market, was severely limited. It was necessary to do considerable research in order to determine appropriate administrative policies, such as the wage-rate bracket approach to correct interplant inequities or the job evaluation approach to correct intraplant inequities, as well as to process particular cases which came before it. Besides its own sizable staff, the board made extensive use of the Bureau of Labor Statistics for field wage surveys and to establish measures of the effectiveness of the wage stabilization program.

In addition to investigating and analyzing wage structures, the board also conducted several interesting studies of the effects of its wage decisions upon specific labor markets in order to assess the validity of its guiding policies. The research division of the board also carried on extensive reviews of board decisions in dispute cases to illuminate the general policies evolving out of the case-by-case common law approach and thereby provide guides for the regional boards and industry agencies of the board, as well as for the unions and employers who were ruled by them.

During the war, the consumers price index of the Bureau of Labor Statistics became a major tool of governmental economic stabilization policy and, inevitably, a subject of considerable controversy. The unions in particular contended that the index understated the true rise in prices and thereby unfairly limited permissible wage increases. As a result of the controversy, the NWLB felt impelled to appoint a committee of outstanding economists and statisticians to make a detailed study of the index and its applicability to wartime economic policies. The report that this study yielded led to a number of changes in the construction and interpretation of the index.

The types of research described above were paralleled in the manpower field by the War Manpower Commission. As in the case of wages, it was soon found that knowledge about occupations, labor mobility, and labor resources was extremely limited and a great deal of basic fact-finding and analysis was required. Likewise, the commission discovered that research was essential to enable it to formulate rules regulating manpower and to develop programs that would provide the needed employees for the critical war industries.

Since the end of the war, the use of research as a tool of policy-making and administration in the labor field has become common practice. Again, a few examples may be illustrative. In 1962, the BLS was instructed by Congress to make an annual survey of the salaries and fringe benefits of clerical, technical, professional, and administrative employees in private industry throughout the nation so that the government could establish a systematic procedure for comparable payments to Civil Service employees. For many years the BLS had made occupational and industry surveys for the use of private employers and unions, and in the process its staff had become highly proficient in the conduct of such surveys. The new responsibility given it by Congress symbolized the public confidence that it had achieved. The productivity studies of the bureau in connection with the wage guidepost policy and its manpower studies have also had a significant impact on government policy-making.

Another agency of the Department of Labor, the Office of Manpower, Automation, and Training (renamed the Office of Manpower Policy, Evaluation, and Research in 1966) has contracted out much of the research which it deems desirable to carry out its function of "developing information and methods needed to deal with the problems of unemployment." Some of the projects are assigned to other governmental units, such as the BLS and the Bureau of the Census. Many of the projects are carried out by university and other academic institutions, some at the specific request of OMAT, others upon submission of a project proposal. The resort to contracting, which has been used on a smaller scale by other Department of Labor agencies, including even the BLS to a minor degree, is a reflection of the extraordinary expansion in labor programs, the expanded funds available for research, and the limited supply of trained researchers on the government payroll.

Still another illustration of administrative research may be found in the developing program of the Equal Employment Opportunity Commission, which was created under Title VII of the 1964 Civil Rights Act to prevent discrimination in private employment because of race, color, religion, sex, or national origin. A letter from the head of its Office of Technical Studies noted that the commission was "asking the social science research community to assist us in undertaking a sustained systematic inquiry into the dynamics of equal employment opportunity. A preliminary step is to compile an inventory of relevant research, both in progress and already completed, on employment opportunity and the economic aspects of race relations. Later we shall be concerned with redefining concepts, examining methodologies, and analyzing employment patterns and practices."

The changing complexion of governmental interests

in labor research is well depicted in some remarks by Arthur M. Ross upon being sworn in as Commissioner of Labor Statistics in October, 1965. Ross first noted the long-standing programs of the bureau beginning with strikes in 1881, productivity in 1894, wholesale prices in 1902, retail food prices and occupational wages in 1903, union wage rates in 1908, and standard budgets in 1909. He then pointed to the escalating economic, social, and technological changes of recent years and the resultant need "for new initiatives" by the BLS, already noted in Chapter 1. Among the specific areas in which Ross felt more intensive research was needed were "the new dimensions of the economy and the labor force," specifically the white-collar, technical, and professional occupations and the mercantile, financial, educational, governmental, and other so-called tertiary activities. Whereas in earlier decades the nation was preoccupied with "industrial injuries, endemic labor turnover, labor-management conflicts, mass unemployment, etc.," the crucial issues of today were "manpower development, equal employment opportunity, eradication of poverty, protection of consumers, and expansion of foreign trade. . . . The BLS has much to contribute toward the formulation of policies and the evaluation of results in all these fields."

Research for Management

Administrative research seems to have been performed on a larger scale for government than for either corporations or unions. Nevertheless, the developments in corporations and unions warrant attention. Corporate labor research goes back to the pioneering studies of Henry R. Towne, Frederick

Taylor, and the other early students of scientific management active between 1886 and 1910. These men were largely engineers by training, and their principal professional organization was the American Society of Mechanical Engineers. In 1912, they founded the Society to Promote the Science of Management, renamed the Taylor Society after Taylor's death in 1915, and which in 1934 became the Society for the Advancement of Management. An examination of the sixteen articles on industrial management published in the *Transactions* of the ASME, from Towne's 1886 paper on "The Engineer as an Economist" to H. L. Gantt's 1908 paper on "Training Workmen in Habits of Industry and Cooperation," reveals that the primary preoccupations of this group were how to motivate workers to work harder and more efficiently and how to allocate and arrange work on a more scientific basis. Wage incentive systems, time study, and work methods were the subjects of in-plant research and experimentation. However, as an ASME report on "The Present State of the Art of Industrial Management" in 1912 stated:

. . . the most important change . . . is in the mental attitude toward the problems of production. The tendency is toward an attitude of questioning, of research, of careful investigation of everything affecting the problems in hand, of seeking for exact knowledge and then shaping action on the discovered facts. It has developed the use of time study and motion study as instruments for investigation, the planning department as an agency to put into practice the conclusions drawn from the results of research, and methods of wage payments which stimulate cooperation.[6]

The industrial engineers of the first decade of the century also played an important role in the development of the "safety-first" movement, which was

adopted by numerous industries as a result of growing public criticism of industrial accidents as well
as the enactment of workmen's compensation laws. In
order to reduce the economic and social costs of accidents, engineers carried out numerous research
studies and helped develop what L. P. Alford has
referred to as

a large body of practice in regard to safeguarding machinery
and working spaces, establishing and operating first-aid
rooms and factory hospitals, toward improving the heating,
ventilation and sanitary conditions in factories, removing
or mitigating conditions tending toward occupational disease, providing medical, dental and nursing service for the
families of employees, establishing medical examinations
before employment and at stated intervals thereafter,
teaching personal hygiene to employees and their families,
and, in fact, a complete new outlook in regard to the health
and physical welfare of all who are engaged in industry.[7]

The next important development in industrial labor
research, which was at least partly influenced by the
scientific management movement, dealt with psychological testing for selection and placement of employees. A concern to reduce the high costs of labor
turnover was another motivating factor. Between 1912
and 1915, the pioneers of industrial psychology, Hugo
Munsterberg of Harvard, Walter D. Scott of North-
western, and Walter V. Bingham of the Carnegie
Institute of Technology, set the stage for the formulation and application of selection tests in industry and
business that rapidly took hold among both the professional psychologists and the leaders of the business
world. The widely publicized findings of the Army
intelligence tests during World War I gave added
impetus to this movement, and after the war the con-

sulting psychologist as well as the full-time corporation psychologist became a common phenomenon, even something of a fad. Although this faddist bubble burst in the second half of the twenties, applied psychology as an instrument of industrial management had become firmly entrenched.[8]

An even more important development on the research front in industry emerged from the celebrated studies at the Hawthorne plant of the Western Electric Company between 1924 and 1931. Influenced by British wartime studies of hours, fatigue, and productivity, this research began with a focus on the connection between physical work conditions, such as lighting and heat, and employee efficiency. Negative and ambiguous findings from experiments with these variables led to observation of the social and psychological characteristics and behavior of the work groups, the attitudes of individual workers, and the role of leadership. The second phase of the Hawthorne studies was carried on by a team of company personnel men and a number of students and associates of Elton Mayo of Harvard. The writings by Mayo and his colleagues became the basis of the "human relations in industry" approach, which strongly influenced personnel programs for at least a decade and a half following World War II and which, in a more sophisticated combination with aspects of scientific management, is still the dominant element in management's relations with employees.

An interest in employee attitudes, job satisfaction, and morale had preceded the Hawthorne studies. Thus, a number of psychological consulting firms, like Houser Associates and the Psychological Corporation, as well as companies like Procter and Gamble and Sears, Roebuck, made attitude surveys during the

1920's and 1930's. However, the reports on Hawthorne gave a great boost to this type of industrial inquiry—especially in the post-World War II period. The most common technique has been the sample survey, using questionnaires or interviews, of the type popularized by the Gallup and Roper opinion survey organizations or the more refined type developed by the Survey Research Center of the University of Michigan under the leadership of Rensis Likert and Angus Campbell. A more unusual approach is illustrated by the General Motors essay contest sponsored in 1949 on "My Job and Why I Like It."

During the past decade, the uses of employee-related research by industry have broadened. At General Electric, for example, personnel psychologists have studied the interests of workers in different types of benefit programs as a basis for developing alternatives from among which choices could be made. At Westinghouse, as an aftermath to a lengthy strike over wage incentives, a private research organization, Industrial Relations Counsellors, was employed to investigate the wage payment system. The Armour Automation Commission, a joint union-management body, sponsored a series of studies on the effects of the company's shutdown of several obsolete plants on the displaced employees and what might be done to relocate their former employees. International Business Machines researchers have investigated the reactions of employees to the introduction of a work measurement program. Sears, Roebuck and Company has studied the relations between organizational size and structure and employee attitudes. A number of major corporations have devoted considerable attention to the problem of identifying in advance high-potential executives. Communications is another subject of corporate research interest. These are only a few examples of a trend which is certain to accelerate, although the positive impact of such research on productivity, efficiency, employee satisfaction, or profitability is difficult to evaluate.

Research for Unions

Although labor leaders were in the forefront of the movement to establish state and federal bureaus of labor statistics in the nineteenth century, the unions did not establish their own research departments until after World War I. During the 1902 anthracite coal dispute, John R. Commons did some research for John Mitchell, the union president; and other unions were occasionally aided in the same way. The Amalgamated Clothing Workers, with Leo Wolman as their research head, and the International Brotherhood of Electrical Workers, with Marion Hedges as research director, were pioneers. The printing unions have long conducted research on work methods and machines. During the 1920's, a group of intellectuals who were highly sympathetic to the labor unions also established private labor research bureaus in New York, Chicago, Boston, Cleveland, Washington, and San Francisco to do research for labor on a contract basis. The AFL employed a professional engineer to work on problems related to scientific management.

The NRA codes gave union research a stimulus comparable to that given to the government. In order to be able to participate effectively in the framing of the codes, the unions needed competent economists to prepare their briefs. Participation in Congressional hearings, while not new, had a similar impact. With the growth of the New Deal labor agencies, such as the National Labor Relations Board, the Wage and Hour and Public Contracts Division, and the Social Security Administration, systematic data analysis by union staffs became essential. Statisticians, economists, accountants, and lawyers were added to the payrolls of a sizable number of international unions as well as the AFL and later the CIO. The tremendous expansion in unionization and collective bargaining gave a further boost to union research activities, both in connection with organizing drives and contract negotiations. This impetus, in turn, was followed by the stimuli of the wage stabilization, dispute settlement, and manpower control programs of World War II. It became virtually impossible for a union to function without professional staff assistance, much of which involved some form of research.

Since the end of the war, the increasing institutionalization of labor relations—reflected in the almost universal use of grievance arbitration, the formulation and evaluation of fringe benefits, the difficult adjustments to technological change, the increasing involvement of labor in political action and community affairs, and the widening interest of the unions in domestic and international affairs—has intensified labor's research needs.

In 1950, it was reported that 39 of the AFL's 107 affiliates had research departments and 12 others combined research with education; 22 of the CIO's 33 affiliates had research departments and 7 others combined research with education; and 20 of 69 independent unions had research departments with 8 others in combination form. The research staffs varied in size from 21 to 1, the major units being the Auto Workers (21), the Machinists (15), the Textile Workers, CIO (15), the Teamsters (14), the Amalgamated

Clothing Workers (13), the Ladies Garment Workers (8), and the Steelworkers (5–9).[9]

A survey by the Bureau of Labor Statistics in 1964 found 118 out of 189 reporting national unions with research directors. Of these, 101 were persons other than the president or secretary-treasurer. In 53 of the 101 cases, the research director was also in charge of education. In addition, 14 state labor organizations reported research directors, of whom 7 were not the president or secretary-treasurer. No data were available on the total number of professionally trained researchers.[10]

Although much union research is of a rather routine nature, such as the compiling of statistical and economic data from published sources or the classification and analysis of contract clauses, some unions have undertaken or sponsored research of a sophisticated nature comparable in quality to the best in government and industry. Solomon Barkin, for over twenty-five years research director of the Textile Workers Union of America, has described how his union, in cooperation with the BLS, in 1944, undertook to demonstrate to the War Labor Board the need for a change in the board's definition of substandard wages. The extensive research included field surveys of textile worker family budgets, the incomes and financial obligations of textile families, and the general economic plight of the textile workers in comparison with other workers, as well as the amassing and analysis of a voluminous record of documentary data on the economics of the industry.[11] A more limited survey, which, however, proved to be highly useful to the officers of the union for organizing and administrative purposes, was done by the Printing Pressmen's Union on how well the union had organized

craft members in the commercial printing and newspaper publishing industries as well as other groups in
the organization's jurisdiction.[12] Among the studies
carried out by the American Federation of Teachers
has been an annual survey of teachers' salaries from
school districts with population of 10,000 or over, an
analysis of state tenure laws, and a study of local
union problems and practices with respect to discipline in the schools.[13] The Pulp and Sulphite Workers Union, like many others, has made a study of the
patterns and rates of expansion in its industry compared with other industries.[14]

As in the case of industry, it is not uncommon for
unions to use the services of outside research organizations (private, academic, or government) when their
own staff resources are limited or when the imprint
of objectivity is strategically important. The Steelworkers Union, for example, used economist Robert
Nathan and his associates to prepare elaborate economic briefs in several of their national negotiations.
The same union engaged one of the nation's leading
specialists on guaranteed annual wage plans, Murray
W. Latimer, to prepare a report for them when this became a major issue. In a number of cases, unions have
also financed surveys of their members' attitudes toward various union policies and programs. One well-
known study of this type was carried out by a research
team at the University of Illinois for District 9 of
the Machinists' Union.[15]

Despite the activities portrayed above, both corporate and union research has been far more limited
in scope and depth than conditions would appear to
justify. The reasons for these limitations relate in part
to misconceptions of what social science can and should
contribute to administrators and in part to the con-

ceptual and methodological inadequacies of social science research. These reasons will be discussed further in a later chapter. Both past trends and current conditions, however, point to the continuing expansion of research for labor administration.

IV   *Toward the Development of a Science*

Research of a purely empirical character is essential to the development of an academic field in its early stages. However, if the field is to continue to progress, it must develop a body of concepts, principles, and theories that will facilitate generalization and stimulate the creation of new hypotheses for further study. Recognition of this need was expressed by the pioneers of the field.

In an introduction to one of the volumes in the distinguished series of the Johns Hopkins' monographs on labor, published in 1906, Jacob Hollander, after paying tribute to the great researches of Beatrice and Sidney Webb in Britain, wrote:

If the economic investigator—and, in particular, the economic investigator in the United States—is to attain his highest scientific possibility, he must realize more fully than heretofore that there is no short cut to economic knowledge. He must adopt a mode analogous to that employed by the physical scientist and described as extensive or experimental, rather than intensive or institutional. He must derive his subject matter not from history alone, nor from the present experience of restricted localities; but he must observe and collate the phenomena under consideration from an area practically coextensive with their manifestation; he must interpret each group of facts in the light of conditions prevailing in the particular place; and he must test the uniformities revealed by reference, as tentative hypotheses, to conditions in still other localities.[1]

Ely, Commons, Hoxie, and other labor economists of the period would have taken issue with Hollander on his rejection of the institutional approach, but they would have agreed wholeheartedly with this view of the study of labor as social science. Equally positive statements of this view were offered by leaders of the movement to solve the problems of labor and industry through engineering and psychological frameworks (e.g., Frederick Taylor and Hugo Munsterberg). Thus, it may reasonably be concluded that the study by Americans of both labor and management as scientific subjects took firm root during the first decade of the twentieth century.

There is, of course, no one route in the development of a science. In the labor-management field at least five different routes may be identified: the statistical, the historical-institutional, the sociopsychological, the experimental, and the model-building. The description and analysis of these approaches may be aided by focusing on the individuals who have been their outstanding exponents. For the most part, attention in this chapter will be directed to developments prior to World War II; the model-building approach will require postwar references because of its relatively recent rise to prominence.

The Statistical Approach

The statistical approach (as a general orientation and not merely the use of statistical methods) came first and is perhaps best illustrated in the work of Carroll D. Wright, which has already been discussed. In testifying before the U.S. Industrial Commission in 1898, Wright commented:

Statistics prove absolutely the improvement in the social and economic condition of the wage earner during the past twenty years. Philosophy, from a socialistic point of view, assumes the reverse of that; but I am in the habit of adhering to the statistical point of view, although that does not always show underlying conditions and the psychological conditions underlying an economic question. Why a thing is done does not conform very well to the statistical method. What is done is generally obtained in that way.[2]

As one of the pioneers in the development of labor statistics, Wright was strongly motivated to persuade the general public, as well as economists and other social scientists, that statistics had an important contribution to make. Addressing social scientists in 1895, he noted that the *bête noire* of the student of social science was insufficient information, and that the statistical information provided by the federal government was indispensable for scientific discussion of the social problems of the day. Wright did not wish to have the government statistician become either a policy-maker or a theorist. He believed, however, that scientifically gathered statistics were essential to the scientific study of society. This view was clearly reflected in the following portrayal of the social scientist, expressed in the simplistic terms of late nineteenth-century positivism:

The student of social science cannot be a partisan; he must accept conclusions which are proved. He may advocate reforms, he may insist upon changes in legislation, upon the adoption of new systems of finance or commerce, but he does all this because to his mind the ascertained facts lead to his conclusions, and until they are completely overturned he will adhere and must adhere to his position; yet he knows well that statistical statements are open to much criticism, and that the results of any governmental inquiry are open to the charge of inadequacy, even when the integrity of the inquiry cannot be questioned in the least. He uses the results of statistical inquiry because the method of obtaining and presenting them is scientific . . . and that if he wishes to grow with advancing history and keep himself fully and thoroughly informed of progress in every direction, he must use the statistical or historical method; and if he is well advanced in his studies the student of social science will use statistical results most critically and with a power of analysis which will enable him at once to see the harmonies involved by which he will accept the true and reject the false.[3]

How far the social scientist had to go was demonstrated by Wright as he traced the evolution of wage statistics.[4] One of the major problems of the state and federal bureaus of labor statistics during the nineteenth century was how to compute proper averages of wages for different classes of work, different industries, and the working population as a whole. Wright noted with some pride that the first frequency distribution of earnings by occupation appeared in the third annual report of the Massachusetts Bureau in 1872, although it was not used on a regular basis until 1884. The issue of unweighted versus weighted averages was in the early stage of discussion. Index numbers of any kind were not to be computed on a regular basis in the United States until Bradstreet's

price series in 1897, and the first continuing government price series was that of the U.S. Department of
Labor in 1902.[5] Serious concern about sampling did
not emerge until the 1930's.

The statistical method was successfully pursued by
academicians in a number of important branches of
the labor field of which wages, strikes, and union membership may be illustrative. An outstanding example
in the wage area was Paul Douglas, whose study of
real wages in the United States between 1890 and 1926
provided strong support for the neoclassical marginal
productivity theory of wages.[6] Douglas' basic data
came from governmental sources. So, too, John I.
Griffin's analysis of strike statistics through 1936 was
based on federal and state compilations, and Griffin's
excellent survey of the literature reveals that his
predecessors were equally indebted to governmental
agencies.[7] On the other hand, the work of Leo Wolman on union membership, sponsored by the National
Bureau of Economic Research, involved an original
collection of data through questionnaires and analysis
of union convention proceedings.[8] Wolman's scholarly
and exacting methodology made his studies the standard work on the subject and, like the work of the
NBER in the fields of national income and business
cycles, they have had a significant impact on the data-
gathering activities of the federal government.

The Historical-Institutional Approach

The historical-institutional studies of Commons and
his students remain, to this day, among the most important contributions to knowledge in the labor field,
although a growing number of recent monographic
studies are modifying, replacing, and supplementing

their findings. Were this activity not occurring, we would be bound to conclude that the field no longer merited the interest of the social scientist. Commons was not interested in history simply as the recounting of a past story. Rather, he sought through history to explain how present institutions had evolved and to help predict the course of future developments. This objective is illustrated by his study of the "American Shoemakers, 1648–1895," in which, like an archeologist, he "reconstructed" a series of stages of industrial development and showed how the ever-widening area of product and labor competition brought forth protective organizations and policies on the part of both employers and employees to ward off the "unfair" menaces to their economic positions.[9] Unfortunately, no one has attempted to replicate Commons' study in other industries and thereby to test the validity of his conclusions, although Lloyd Ulman's investigation into the rise of the national trade union during the nineteenth century in five crafts comes close to doing so, and seriously challenges some of Commons' major generalizations.[10]

The four-volume *History of Labor in the United States,* which covers the period from colonial days to 1932, was primarily concerned with the evolution of the labor movement's philosophies, ideologies, programs, and policies in the nation's economic and political spheres. Its major contribution was to explain the hardiness and survival ability of business or job-conscious unionism in a hostile environment. Selig Perlman's *A Theory of the Labor Movement,* undoubtedly the single most influential work of its kind in the field, was the culmination of this historical research.[11]

As a natural concomitant of his historical research,

Commons also conducted and directed research into contemporary forms of industrial government. Some of his earliest studies covered the longshoremen of the Great Lakes, the musicians of St. Louis and New York, the steelworkers of Pittsburgh, and the coal miners. Shortly after World War I, he made what was probably the first and, for many years, certainly the largest comparative analysis of the different forms of industrial government in some thirty enterprises. Collective bargaining, profit sharing, shop committees, scientific management, boards of arbitration, and other types of relations were scrutinized and compared.[12]

In his delightful autobiography, *Myself,* written at the age of seventy, Commons recalled that it was in 1903, when he was leading a survey into restrictive practices of labor and capital for the Department of Labor, that discussions with Ethelbert Stewart, one of his colleagues, led him to develop the " 'academic' general principles underlying unionism and collective bargaining," which ultimately became a major theme of his institutional economics.[13] The theoretical framework of institutional economics—an ambitious effort to formulate a general theory of economic action—did not attract the wide interest of Perlman's theory, but it reflected Commons' deep concern with the development of social science, as well as with research for administration.

A second major stream of historical-institutional studies was produced at Johns Hopkins University under the leadership first of Richard Ely and later of Jacob Hollander and George Barnett. Barnett's own studies of the printers, technological change, and multiunit collective bargaining are among the classics of the field. The distinctive contribution of the Johns Hopkins group, however, was the series of investigations into the structure and policies of the national unions, thereby complementing the Wisconsin studies of labor ideologies.

The two other major centers of academic research in the labor field prior to World War II, the University of Chicago and Columbia University, were also largely oriented to the institutional approach. At Chicago, under the direction of Harry A. Millis, a Commons student during Commons' early Indiana period, important studies of the development of collective bargaining and of the government's impact on it were made by Harry Wolf (on the Railroad Labor Board), Royal Montgomery (on the Chicago building trades), Carroll Christenson (on Chicago labor relations), and Emily C. Brown (on book and job printing). At Columbia, studies by Paul Brissenden on the Industrial Workers of the World, Elizabeth Baker on commercial printing labor, Edward Berman on labor disputes and the President of the United States, and Vincent Lanfear on business fluctuations and the labor movement reflected a similar approach.

Sociopsychological Approaches

A number of unrelated institutionalists, influenced by Thorstein Veblen rather than by Commons, adopted a somewhat different focus. They might be called the sociopsychological group, although they were trained neither as sociologists nor psychologists. Robert F. Hoxie and Carleton Parker are its most distinguished examples.

Hoxie saw unionism as the outgrowth of social psychology. Workers who are "similarly situated economically and socially, closely associated and not too divergent in temperament and training, will tend to

develop a common interpretation of the social situation
and a common solution of the problem of living.
This may come about gradually and spontaneously, or
it may be the apparently sudden outcome of some
crisis in the lives of the men concerned. . . . But whatever the immediate cause, the result is the same. A
social group is thus constituted, marked off by a more
or less unified and well-developed but effective view-
point or group psychology."[14] Thus, there was no
single form, or type, of unionism. Nor was unionism,
in the broad sense of the word, confined to wage-
workers. "It may exist wherever in society there is a
group of men with consciousness of common needs and
interests apart from the rest of society." Employers,
merchants, farmers, and professional men all had their
own unions.

With this orientation, it is not surprising that Hoxie
trained his students at the University of Chicago to
investigate the "aims, principles and theories, policies,
demands, methods, and attitudes of trade unionism,"
as well as to observe objective behavior. Hoxie's own
major research project—the study of scientific management and labor for the U.S. Commission on Industrial Relations in 1914–1915—brilliantly reflected
his wide-ranging approach. In his autobiography,
Commons wrote that neither before nor since had he
ever seen as comprehensive and detailed an outline
of an investigation as the one submitted by Hoxie.[15]

Like Hoxie, Carleton Parker had a very limited
body of publications during his relatively short life
(he died at age forty, Hoxie at forty-eight), but he
was more intimately acquainted, through personal
observation and study, with the IWW than any other
academician. In the brief series of articles compiled
by his wife after his death, he explained and demon-

strated why, after teaching labor problems for three years and studying the subject in two American universities, under Sidney Webb in England, and at four German universities, he had concluded that economic principles were totally inadequate to interpret the behavior of the migratory farm worker in California and that only a study of Freud and other writers in abnormal and behavioristic psychology had led him in the "right" direction. He concluded: "So the problem of industrial labor is one with the problem of the discontented business man, the indifferent student, the unhappy wife, the immoral minister—it is one of mal-adjustment between a fixed human nature and a carelessly ordered world."[16] Parker's psychology, with its emphasis on "innate and unsuppressible tendencies" or instincts, soon lost its appeal. His insights into the unrest of migratory labor, however, remain a part of the permanent literature in the field.

The application of the principles of social psychology to labor problems by economists like Hoxie, Parker, and Commons himself (with his negotiational psychology), was inevitably taken over by professionally trained sociologists and psychologists who had no contact with the former and were uninfluenced by them. Elton Mayo and his Harvard Business School associates were among the first prominent noneconomists to concentrate on labor problems outside of the testing, selection, and training area. Employee attitude and morale studies were undertaken by a few psychologists in the 1920's and early 1930's of whom J. David Houser and Arthur Kornhauser were important examples. Alfred W. Jones' study of the attitudes of a sizable cross section of Akron residents toward "life, liberty, and property" as related to the controversial rubber industry situation of the 1930's reflected the increasing sophistication of psychological research techniques. The flood of attitude research was not to come until World War II and its aftermath, but the growing interest of psychologists and their potential contribution to scientific knowledge in the labor field was shown in the formation of the Society for the Psychological Study of Social Issues in 1936 as a division of the American Psychological Association. The first publication of the society, in 1939, dealt with the subject of industrial conflict. The contributions of the sociopsychological approach to the study of labor since World War II will be discussed in the next chapter.

Social Experimentation

Another route to the development of a science of labor relations is found in the work of the experimentalists, who believed that the methods that had proved so successful in the physical and biological sciences could be adapted by the social sciences with equal success. The pioneering figure in this area is Frederick Taylor, whose experiments with time study and work measurement within industry in the 1880's were followed by similar experiments in both real work situations and laboratory experiments. Taylor describes in engaging fashion how the president of the Midvale Steel Company, for which he had been working as foreman, gave approval to his desire for experimentation "more as a reward for having, to a certain extent, 'made good' as foreman of the shop in getting more work out of men, than for any other reason":

Among several investigations which were undertaken at this time, one was an attempt to find some rule, or law, which would enable a foreman to know in advance how much of any kind of heavy laboring work a man who was well suited to his job ought to do in a day; that is, to study the tiring effect of heavy labor upon a first-class man. Our first step was to employ a young college graduate to look up all that had been written on the subject in English, German, and French. Two classes of experiments had been made; one by physiologists who were studying the endurance of the human animal, and the other by engineers who wished to determine what fraction of a horse-power a man-power was. . . . However, the records of these investigations were so meager that no law of any value could be deduced from them. We therefore started a series of experiments of our own.[17]

The Hawthorne experiments at the Western Electric Company in the 1920's also started with an engineering approach to ascertain the relationship between the productivity of assembly workers and the physical conditions of work, such as lighting and ventilation. By holding constant as many conditions as possible and varying one factor at a time, the Hawthorne experimenters hoped to discover the types of generalizations that Taylor had been seeking forty years earlier. As often happens in experiments, surprising results of not only a negative but even an inverse relation to what was expected, led to the insight that the sociopsychological character of the small work group was a key to the problem of work performance. Out of further experiments based on this insight, Elton Mayo and his associates moved into the more clinical approach of nondirective interviewing and the study of attitudes.[18]

Despite the international acclaim given to the Hawthorne studies, the experimental approach has not played a major role in the subsequent development of industrial relations as a scientific discipline. "Field" experimentation has been confined, for the most part, to small groups within a few factories, dealing with problems of productivity, group cohesiveness or morale, leadership, and the innovation of technological or organizational change. Followers of Kurt Lewin, influenced by his important laboratory experiments with groups of children in democratic and autocratic atmospheres, conducted a series of experiments at the sewing plant of the Harwood Manufacturing Corporation in Virginia, in which democratic techniques were used to increase worker productivity.[19] Another Harwood experiment involved democratic participation in deciding upon changes in job methods. The Research Center for Group Dynamics at the University of Michigan, grounded in Lewinian theory, has probably contributed more to industrial relations through its field and laboratory experiments than any other single institution using similar techniques. Laboratory and simulation experiments, however, are widely practiced by psychologists throughout the country on basic sociopsychological themes (e.g., learning, perception, motivation, and bargaining), which may ultimately have important influence on the field, although thus far the effects have been limited.

Model-Building and Testing

The last of the five approaches to the development of a science of industrial relations is at once one of the oldest and the most recent. Theoretical model-building, using geometric or algebraic language, has been a tool of economists since the early nineteenth century, but its use as a systematic tool of empirical research in the labor field is essentially a post-World War II phenomenon. For the most part, it relies on regression analysis of statistical data gathered to test particular hypotheses from the models that are expressed as algebraic equations. Its application by labor economists has been chiefly in the areas of manpower allocation, investment in human capital, and wages. As examples in the manpower field, reference may be made to the work of Clarence D. Long on the labor force, Jacob Mincer on married women workers, and Lee Hansen on the cycloid sensitivity of the labor supply.[20] In the human investment field, dealing with social expenditures on education, training, and health, the recent work of Gary Becker is particularly well-known.[21] Finally, in the wage area, we may cite the pioneering writings of Paul Douglas, as well as that of a younger scholar like Walter A. Fogel.[22] Because of the recency of most of this work, it is too early to judge how important it will be in the development of general principles of labor.

Thanks in part to the development of operations research, students of organization behavior, and particularly of organization decision-making, have also been using models as a basis for the generation of hypotheses to be tested empirically. However, the primary subject of this method has been the management organization, from the standpoint of the manager. Union organizations have been largely ignored, and bilateral bargaining models have been confined to theory or to laboratory experimentation.

Whether industrial relations can be treated as a separate discipline is still a debatable subject, but there is no doubt that the advance of the social sciences in general, and particularly of what has come to be labeled the behavioral sciences, has significant

implications for the development of industrial relations as a field of scientific study. In the two decades
since the end of World War II, progress in conceptualization as well as methodology in nonlabor areas
has greatly aided students of labor problems. Thus,
the scientific study of labor problems has benefited
both from internal developments and from external
sources, much as the fields of medicine and engineering.

V ___ Expanding Knowledge and Current Gaps

The evolution of research in labor problems in terms of three main motives—the reform of society, the improvement of administration, and the development of a science—has already been delineated. Here, attention is directed to the major subject areas of the field in order to depict both the progress that has been made in increasing knowledge and resolving problems and the questions that have remained unanswered either because they have been slighted or ineffectively investigated. Obviously, it is not possible in a limited space to encompass all of the published research, or even all of the important studies, but enough of the best work can be noted so as to provide a sense of the main lines of development.[1] Although some reference is made to earlier research, the discussion in this chapter is largely devoted to the years since the end of World War II.

The subject matter of the labor field can be subdivided in numerous ways. Seven categories are used here as rough guidelines, with the recognition that a considerable amount of overlap among them is unavoidable:

1. *Labor history*—the study of the development over time of the American labor movement, its aspirations and methods, the problems encountered, and the results achieved.

2. *Union-management relations*—this category includes collective bargaining, grievance handling, dispute settlement, work stoppages, and industrial relations systems in general.

3. *Public policy*—the entire range of public policy-making by legislative, administrative, and judicial bodies with respect to employees and their organizations; and the political activities of labor, employer, and other related interest groups.

4. *The labor market*—this category encompasses much of the research of the labor economists relating to wages and employment, labor mobility, productivity and technological change, labor costs, income security, unemployment, and poverty. It also includes the work of sociologists and psychologists on occupational choice and career development.

5. *Organizational behavior and interpersonal relations*—the study of the structure and internal functioning of industrial and labor organizations; human relations in industry; interpersonal and administrative behavior; the motivations and morale of managers, workers, and labor leaders; and attitudes toward work.

6. *Foreign labor and international comparisons*—the study of foreign labor relations, with particular attention to the implications for the United States of the labor problems in economic development, and of international labor movements and standards.

7. *Industrial society* — the concern of sociologists, anthropologists, and social philosophers with the broad social problems of a technological civilization and the social movements to cope with them.

Labor History

Post-World War II students of labor have devoted less of their resources to historical projects than to other subjects. Since 1945, a number of interesting and important studies have been published, and a new journal, *Labor History,* as well as a new association of labor historians have been founded. But no enterprise comparable to Commons' ten-volume *Documentary History* or to the four volumes of the *History of Labor in the United States* has been completed. The importance of the *Documentary History* was underscored by the issuance of a new edition in 1958, with five new prefaces by prominent historians to each of the major parts. The new edition not only attempted a reappraisal of the original work (generally favorable) but also surveyed the subsequent contributions to the literature on each segment. On the basis of these later contributions revisions of the conclusions of Commons and his associates were presented and debatable or open questions requiring further research were indicated. Perhaps the most significant contemporary development, paralleling the *Documentary History* in some respects, has been the oral history projects at Columbia, California, Wisconsin, and Michigan Universities in which veteran participants in the labor movement, industry, and government have tape-recorded their memories of past experiences. Another impressive but incomplete multi-volume *History of the Labor Movement in the United States* is the Marxist-oriented work of Philip S. Foner, four volumes of which have thus far been published.

The need for a revised history of American labor has been widely recognized, however, as a result of the findings of individual scholars.[2] Richard B. Morris' exhaustive examination of colonial labor records, although begun prior to the war, was published in 1946 and revealed labor events and practices not known to the Commons team. Pre-Civil War studies by Louis H. Arky, William A. Sullivan, and Walter A. Hugins have modified views about labor's early participation in politics, stressing the role of middle-class reformers and businessmen. The post-Civil War literature has been enriched by Lloyd Ulman's comprehensive analysis of the rise of the national trade union and his challenge to Commons' theory, as well as by Charlotte Erickson's and Clifton K. Yearley's studies of European immigrant labor, Gerald N. Grob's reassessment of the Knights of Labor and other reformist movements, and Samuel Bernstein's study of the First International in America.

The monographic materials for a more definitive history of twentieth-century labor have also begun to appear. For the Progressive era and beyond, we now have Marguerite Green's detailed investigation of the National Civic Federation, which, for a few years at the start of the century, raised hopes of a labor-management accommodation; Marc Karson's analysis of labor politics from 1900 to 1918, with particular insights into the Catholic role; a number of illuminating studies of the Jewish labor movement in New York and Chicago; Milton J. Nadworny's survey of scientific management and labor; and industry studies like David Brody's of the steelworkers before they achieved stable unions. The Wilson years, both preceding and during World War I, have been explored quite intensively. On the other hand, the twenties have not yet been examined in the depth they merit, although Irving Bernstein's comprehensive survey has provided some new perspectives on labor's "lean years" in a time of national prosperity. The scholarly assessment of the New Deal years has also started, as witness Walter Galenson's study of the CIO, Sidney Fine's research into the origins of auto unionism in Michigan, the second volume of Philip Taft's history of the AFL (which also covers the 1920's), and we shall soon have Bernstein's continuation of his between-the-wars project.

A variety of interesting historical works worth noting do not readily fit into the above period classification. These include a sizable number of biographies (e.g., of Gompers, Debs, Lewis, and Hoffa), union histories (e.g., the AFL, Machinists, Operating Engineers, Carpenters), and statistical surveys over time (the labor force, wages, productivity, union membership). They also include a sizable body of literature dealing with significant episodes in the history of labor, such as the anthracite coal strike of 1902, the Molly Maguires, and the Seattle general strike. Two highly regarded studies—one about theory[3] and the other about practice[4]—that appeared in the same year are Mark Perlman's *Labor Union Theories in America* and James O. Morris' *Conflict Within the AFL: A Study of Craft Versus Industrial Unionism, 1901–1938.* Reference should also be made to a small but growing body of community labor studies (e.g., Los Angeles, Chicago, Milwaukee, Decatur) and to Archie Green's researches into labor folklore.

Despite this output of historical studies, the postwar years have failed to produce either an overall "new history" or any significant new theory. What is needed is a work that will not only revise Commons' classic on the basis of new data, but will also add new perspectives and insights by broadening and re-integrating its scope. This involves, among other things, a greater recognition of labor developments outside of the mainstream of unionism and labor politics—such as the unorganized blue-collar and white-collar employees, the status and conditions of government and public employees, the Negro labor situation, and farm labor problems. It also calls for utilization of the knowledge accruing from the abundance of recent studies of business organization and policy-making, as well as from the vast bibliography of American social and economic history in general.[5]

Union-Management Relations

In 1939–1940, the Twentieth Century Fund sponsored a comprehensive study of collective bargaining under the direction of Harry A. Millis in which a number of leading students of the subject, together with some younger men, summarized available knowledge on an industry-by-industry basis.[6] It is illuminating to compare this important study with the voluminous postwar research, such as the National Planning Association's "Causes of Industrial Peace," or the volumes by Frederick H. Harbison and Robert Dubin, Harbison and John R. Coleman, William F. Whyte, E. Wight Bakke, Neil W. Chamberlain, Richard A. Lester and Edward A. Robie, Benjamin M. Selekman, Dale Yoder, and the Illini City group at Illinois. Whereas the fund project was industry-oriented, most of the later research focused on the plant, establishment, or company unit. The narrower focus was due in part to the paucity of knowledge at this level, in part to the changed scope of union-management relations, and in part to the recognition that it was essential to get down to the "grass-roots," examining informal as well as formal structure and procedures. Although labor institutionalists have never hesitated to cross disciplinary lines in their investigations, the postwar research reflected a wider and more sophisticated body of concepts, drawing heavily on advances in sociological and psychological disciplines. The study of leader and rank-and-file attitudes, and the probing of their motives and values were combined with the more traditional investigation of organizational activities.

Causal analysis, as opposed to straight description, also attracted much interest. In a few, but not the majority of studies, more systematic and rigorous methodologies were utilized, drawing especially upon advances in sample survey techniques, factor analysis, and nonparametric statistics. One of the major debates among the researchers (led by sociologist Whyte and economist Dunlop) was over the relative importance of in-plant and external environmental factors in determining the quality of plant relations.[7] It was ultimately resolved by general agreement that both were essential. Efforts to assign weights to various determinants, however, did not succeed. Another interesting controversy revolved around the concepts of cooperation and conflict. By the end of the fifties, there was a substantial consensus that the conflict-cooperation continuum was not, by itself, a fruitful avenue to pursue. This judgment was reinforced by the widespread repudiation in management circles of the peace-centered, human-relations value system to which Elton Mayo and his followers had given great stimulus.

Explorations into the meaning and role of power in union-management relations, however, have advanced understanding of worker and union behavior only a small margin beyond the thinking of Commons or Mary Parker Follett.[8] It is true that a considerable amount of speculation about the power concept has been undertaken, but relatively little empirical research about it appears in the literature. One of the most enlightening recent case studies is Ralph and Estelle James' analysis of Jimmy Hoffa as president of the Teamsters Union and the manner in which he obtained and used the power of this great organization—but this is more descriptive of a specific case than generalizable. Neil Chamberlain and James Kuhn contributed the interesting idea of "fractional bargaining" by informal work groups at the shop or departmental level as "a natural development of a power center within, though not necessarily of, the local union."[9] Leonard Sayles and George Strauss, in their studies of local unions, also demonstrated the importance of viewing power as the outcome of diverse, interacting interest groups within the larger institution. Benjamin M. Selekman constructed a system of nine types of union-management relations based on the concept of power. Measurements have been attempted in a few cases, but the various dimensions of power have thus far eluded successful operational treatment in the labor field, and Murray Edelman has concluded that power is not a measurable entity.[10]

The impressive advances of organized labor during the war led the industrial managers to a determination that they must strongly resist further incursion into their managerial domain. Thus, President Truman's postwar conference on labor-management relations in 1945 found the subject of "management rights" a major obstacle to agreement. For academicians, the subject, although not new, naturally became more attractive and interesting. The first important work was Neil Chamberlain's *The Union Challenge to Management Control*,[11] which analyzed union participation in decision-making in terms of the various functions of the management process. At the University of Illinois, Margaret Chandler, W. E. Chalmers, and this author attempted to develop a concept of union influence or participation that could be measured and used as a basis of interplant and interindustry comparison. A recent field study by Chandler of contracting-out has provided an intricate and sophisticated model of the decision-making process in which she traces a variety of labor and management interests, rather than conventionally treating labor and management as homogeneous units. The author has pursued the topic of participation abroad, notably in Britain and Israel, while Adolf Sturmthal has explored it on the European continent. At Harvard, Sumner Slichter, who had made the outstanding prewar study on the subject, together with colleagues James Healy and E. Robert Livernash, surveyed practices of 150 companies in an effort to help "business concerns grow and prosper in the kind of economic environment provided by the American trade union movement."

These and other studies have raised some important questions about the way economic institutions function and the possibilities of further democratization in decision-making (e.g., the idea of "participative management"). An even larger set of questions has been raised by the revival of interest in the concept of "industrial democracy," a subject that attracted much popular and some scholarly attention in the two decades between 1905 and 1925, but which received less emphasis in the next thirty years.

The breaking of new ground at the local level was not matched at higher levels, although the volume of research into industry and national aspects of collective bargaining was substantial. Useful and informative studies, such as the University of Pennsylvania series on industry-wide bargaining and arbitration, and the University of California series on West Coast collective bargaining systems, were traditional in character.

In the realm of theory, two developments are worth noting. John Dunlop formulated a conceptual framework of the "industrial relations system," which bore considerable similarity to Commons'.[12] Dunlop's three main "actors"—managers and their organizations, workers and their organizations, and governmental agencies—paralleled Commons' three main types of collective economic action—the corporations, unions, and political parties. Both men emphasized the conflict of interests and "the working rules" or "web of rules" that were produced by and guided the actors. For Dunlop, environmental conditions were the main determinants of the rules, and he devoted considerable attention to categorizing them under three headings: the technological context, the market or budgetary context, and the power context. Commons, while also very sensitive to environmental factors, as his famous study of economic stages and competitive menaces in the shoe industry demonstrated, analyzed the role of discretionary will, or what he labeled negotiational psychology. Neither framework was a general theory but rather suggested directions for the formulation of such a theory.

The second main development of a theoretical nature reflects an interesting convergence of orthodox economic analysis and institutional thinking and research. In contrast to Dunlop's concern with the more-or-less enduring structure of union-management relations, these writers have focused on the *process* of collective bargaining at a particular point in time. Many of them, especially the orthodox economists, are concerned with the process of wage determination and are endeavoring to make determinate the earlier indeterminate models of John B. Clark, Arthur C. Pigou, John R. Hicks, and others. American writers have been influenced in this area by European scholars like Jan Pen and George L. Shackle, who have given emphasis to the psychological factors of risk-taking, uncertainty, and propensity to fight within the economic framework of bilateral monopoly. Game theory has been another source of stimulation for such model-builders of the bargaining process as Lawrence E. Fouraker, Sidney Siegel, Carl M. Stevens, and Bevars Dupre Mabry, who have been concerned with the application of various strategies. From institutionally oriented labor economists like Ross and Chamberlain have come explorations into the "political" or intraorganizational aspects of union and management decision-making in collective bargaining, as well as numerous empirical studies of bargaining in action. Ideas have been liberally interchanged, so that the pure theorists have a much more sophisticated awareness of reality than many of their forebears, and the institutionalists have been pressed to a more careful and rigorous appraisal of their numerous variables. The bridge between theory and fact, however, has so far defied satisfactory construction. Recently, Richard E. Walton and Robert B. McKersie have made an ambitious effort at integration through a framework based on four subprocesses—distributive bargaining, integrative bargaining, attitudinal structuring tactics, and intraorganizational bargaining tactics—drawing heavily on both theory and empirical research.[13]

One of the weaknesses of the labor field is that the researchers in the mainstream are often poorly informed about or uninterested in the research and writing of scholars in allied or overlapping fields. Thus, with a few exceptions such as the Walton and McKersie study, the literature on union-management relations reflects little of the substantial body of work on conflict resolution, which ranges from the small group to the international scene. Writers like Morton Deutsch who contribute to the *Journal of Conflict Resolution, Human Relations,* or the *Journal of Social Issues,* for example, seem to have few readers among students of union-management relations—a gap in communication that should be closed.

Public Policy

The labor students of pre-World War II were always fascinated by the law. This was perhaps due to the conflicts between property and human rights that were so central to labor relations. Ely wrote on the legal theory of property. Commons not only co-authored one of the standard works on labor legislations, but derived much of his institutional framework from his research into the legal foundations of capitalism. Edwin E. Witte was a drafter of Wisconsin legislation, the chief architect of the federal Social Security law, and author of a major book on the labor injunction. Another Commons student and colleague, Elizabeth Brandeis, became a leading historian of protective labor legislation.

Since 1945, labor institutionalists have devoted less attention to the study of labor law, while legal scholars and political scientists have become much more prominent than before. The political scientists, in the tradition of Arthur Bentley, have been largely concerned with the process of public policy formation and have produced a number of illuminating studies in the labor field. Reference may be made to the work on interest groups by David B. Truman, on political symbolism by Murray Edelman, on the agreed bill process by Gilbert Y. Steiner, on the employment act of 1946 by Stephen K. Bailey, and on workmen's compensation and health insurance by Herman and Anne Somers. Political scientists have also studied the more general political activities of organized labor, such as Fay Calkins' book on the CIO and the Democratic party.

A recent study by Richard C. Cortner of the five cases that determined the constitutionality of the Wagner Act in 1937 is illustrative of the political scientist's orientation. Cortner reveals the complex interplay between the differing interest groups—union, employer, and government—in the passage of the Wagner Act, shows how the National Labor Relations Board's legal staff attempted to set the stage for the testing of the act under the most favorable conditions, and explores how the court revised its interpretation of the commerce clause and the fifth amendment to the federal constitution in the light of changing economic and social conditions and pressures from the White House and other interested groups.[14]

Law professors have likewise come to the fore with important studies of federal labor law, court decisions, the work of administrative agencies, and private arbitration. Archibald Cox has contributed significantly to the understanding of national labor law, Charles O. Gregory to the history of labor law, Benjamin Aaron and Clyde W. Summers to the law of internal union relations, and Robben W. Fleming to the arbitration process and dispute settlement law. The law journals have printed numerous articles and notes on the increasingly complex and comprehensive body of labor law.

Nor have labor economists entirely neglected the field despite the attraction of other problems and subjects. State labor relations legislation was investigated by both Sanford Cohen and Charles C. Killingsworth; Harry A. Millis and Emily C. Brown coauthored the definitive work on the first twelve years of the National Labor Relations Act; Frederic Meyers investigated "right-to-work" legislation in Texas. But these scholars have tended to adhere to conventional methods and concepts rather than break new pathways.

The Labor Market

During World War II, American labor economists and industrial relations specialists, in their roles as wage stabilizers, dispute settlers, and manpower administrators, gained unprecedented insights into the complexities of labor markets and returned to their academic homes with a realization of the vast gaps and serious misconceptions in the technical literature on the subject. As a result, many of the labor economists turned their attention to the twin topics of labor mobility and wage structures, receiving strong stimulus from the Social Science Research Council, which established a labor market research committee in 1946. The capstone of the council's work on labor mobility was the elaborate empirical study, *Labor Mobility in Six Cities,* and a bulletin by Herbert S. Parnes appraising research findings in the United States in the 1930's and 1940's.[15] The bulletin noted that much knowledge had been acquired about the extent of worker mobility from job to job and in and out of the labor market, and the relationship to mobility of such demographic factors as age, race, sex, and marital status. Studies by Charles A. Myers and George P. Shultz, Lloyd G. Reynolds, Murray Edelman, Leonard P. Adams, and others revealed the extreme limitations of worker information about job opportunities and the inadequacies of formal labor market mechanisms, such as the public employment services, in matching supply and demand. Serious doubts were raised about the role of wages in labor allocation theory. The need for further exploration into the motivations and expectations of workers was also underlined, leading to an extensive field study of occupational choice by Gladys L. Palmer, Richard C. Wilcock, Parnes, and others. Throughout this postwar research, the interrelations of psychological and economic variables received particular emphasis.

The wage aspects of the labor market were another major subject of study. Reference has been made above to the work on wage determination, mostly of a short-run nature. A number of important studies were also made of wage structures in an effort to explain longer-run differences in wage payments among occupations, industries, and areas. Lloyd G. Reynolds and associates, for example, investigated wage structures in four American industries and compared the national wage structures of five industrialized nations, including the United States. Wage differentials, with the possible exception of geographical differentials, were found to be diminishing; unionism was shown to be an important equalizing force; union and governmental intervention in the market tended "to supplement and reinforce market tendencies rather than to work against them." Reynolds concluded, as had George W. Taylor and Frank C. Pierson and other labor economists, that an adequate wage theory must integrate the effects of both market and institutional forces, and not treat institutional force as an outside interference.[16] One of the new explanatory concepts in wage analysis was Arthur Ross's "orbits of coercive comparison," which, together with the allied concepts of pattern-setting and pattern-following, received empirical testing by Harold M. Levinson, George Seltzer, and others. A somewhat similar concept was Dunlop's "wage contours." Intraplant or internal wage structures were also studied by Dunlop, E. Robert Livernash, and Jack Stieber, among others.

The impact of unionism on the distribution of national income to the main functional groups in the economy—an old issue—attracted renewed controversy between the general economists, who contended that the unions had no significant effect but, nonetheless, worried deeply about union monopoly power, and the labor economists, who argued that the unions did affect distributive shares although their statistical studies were inconclusive. Clark Kerr concluded, in 1957, that unions can raise labor's share, under certain conditions, but not very much unless there is a significant shift in decision-making power from the employer to the union. In a related subject area, Albert Rees, after a review of further research in 1962, judged that unions have probably had their main impact at the expense of the less skilled and the unorganized. Similarly, H. Gregg Lewis, in the latest and most extensive study of the union impact on relative wages that included a comprehensive survey of the literature, concluded, among other things, that union-ism has increased the inequality of average relative wages among industries by only about 8 per cent and among workers within industries by less than 5 per cent.[17]

The war also stimulated a strong interest in the problem of inflation and, particularly, in the relation between union wages and prices. This interest was intensified by the successive "rounds" of postwar wage increases, leading to a lengthy national debate be-tween the proponents of "cost-push" and "demand-pull" theories until the early 1960's. After the mid-1950's, the growing rate of unemployment in-jected a complicating concern. Both labor and general economists contributed numerous articles and mono-graphs to the debate, arriving at a fairly extensive con-sensus that there were elements of validity in both theories and such a high degree of interdependence between them as to vitiate their separate treatment. The "guideposts" policy of the President's Council of Economic Advisers relating wages and prices to na-tional productivity as a stabilizing device had a mixed reception among economists; it seemed to be generally agreed that the solution for price stabilization and high employment required a primary reliance upon fiscal-monetary remedies rather than on direct or in-direct governmental controls over wages and prices.

A major stimulant to extensive American research and discussion on the relationship between unemploy-ment and wages came from the statistical analyses of an Englishman, A. W. Phillips, which suggested the possibility of a new economic law.[18] Much of this work was done by general economists and econometricians

like Paul A. Samuelson, Robert M. Solow, and G. L.
Perry. Labor economists have also found Phillips'
work exciting, as witness the studies of William G.
Bowen and R. A. Berry reported in *The Review of
Economics and Statistics* (May, 1963), of Robert R.
France in the *Industrial and Labor Relations Review*
(January, 1962), of Phillip Ross in the *Proceedings*
of the Industrial Relations Research Association
(1961), and Robert L. Raimon in the IRRA *Proceedings* (1963). In general, the American studies have
shown a looser connection between unemployment
rates and wage rate changes than the original studies
by Phillips and R. G. Lipsey and have suggested the
need for considering such additional variables as
profit rates and productivity.

Since the mid-1950's, and together with the high
prosperity of the 1960's, labor market research has reflected the growing national interest in the problems
of the unemployed. One problem that boomed into
prominence after a rather lengthy period of quiet
growth was that of the older worker, especially the
older worker who had lost his job for reasons beyond
his control. The initial interest was reflected in the
first research symposium published, in 1950, by the
IRRA in which economists, medical scientists, sociologists, and psychologists pooled their ideas, facts,
and questions on *The Aged and Society*. The Twentieth Century Fund soon afterward sponsored a substantial study by John J. Corson and John W.
McConnell on economic aspects of retirement. In rather
short order, a number of sizable field studies were
undertaken at the University of California (Margaret
Gordon, *et al.*), at the University of Illinois (Richard
C. Wilcock and Walter Franke), by the Bureau of
Employment Security, and by others. Wilcock and

Irvin Sobel of Washington University directed a survey of forty public employment offices in six states exploring the job placement services for older workers. In combination, these studies helped to undermine many false beliefs about the declining efficiency and reliability of older workers that had been used to buttress the discriminatory practices of employers. They also suggested ways in which older workers might be helped to regain employment and to prepare for retirement.

Another problem that assumed major proportions after 1957 was the controversy over whether the persistent and, for several years, growing unemployment rate was due to inadequate overall growth of the economy or to the structural dislocations of an increasingly complex society. The writings of Charles Killingsworth, Norman J. Simler, and Robert A. Gordon focused on the structural unemployment thesis. The Special Committee on Unemployment Problems of the U.S. Senate, appointed in September, 1959, called on academicians to present their knowledge and theories to the policy-makers.[19] Government funds became a powerful force for research and writing, especially after the election of President Kennedy and the enactment of the Area Redevelopment Act of 1961 and the Manpower Development and Training Act of 1962. The studies of William H. Miernyk, Jacob J. Kaufman and H. J. Golatz on depressed areas may be noted as examples of work connected with these developments.

Research on the characteristics of the unemployed by both government agencies and university scholars (e.g., William G. Bowen and J. A. Finegan) has produced a vast assemblage of facts and has contributed to both public and private policy-making. A series of studies by Richard C. Wilcock and Walter Franke traced and assessed the special job-finding problems of different categories of workers involved in plant shutdowns. More recently, attention has shifted to the problems of retraining workers whose skills have become obsolete and of vocational and technical training for the culturally disadvantaged—mainly Negroes, but also poor whites in large city slums and depressed areas like Appalachia. The cost-benefit analyses of Gerald G. Somers and Ernst W. Stromsdorfer on retraining programs are illustrative of this shift. Negro job status has become a subject of special interest with the rise of the civil rights movement. At the other end of the spectrum is the rising interest in the development of high-level manpower (notably scientists, engineers, and administrators), of which the Princeton studies by Frederick H. Harbison and associates are interesting examples.

About the same time that the labor specialists were broadening their attack on manpower problems, a number of general economists were developing out of economic growth theory a new focus (for purpose of manpower planning) on investment in human resources through education, health, and training. The traditional concepts of capital and capital formation were extended to include human capital. The new concepts, however, were closely integrated with orthodox economic theory in contrast to the earlier institutional approach. Leaders of this approach include older scholars like Theodore W. Schultz and Simon Kuznets and younger economists like Gary Becker, Jacob Mincer, Lee Hansen, and Burton A. Weisbrod. The rapid expansion of interest in recent years suggests that this sector may become one of the important meeting grounds of general economists and labor specialists.

One of the most talked-about "causes" of structural unemployment is rapid technological change, including significant developments in automated equipment with computer controls and feedback mechanisms. Until fairly recently, however, research on this subject was disappointing both in quantity and quality. The best work concerned the adjustment process of the existing labor force to the introduction of automated equipment, and much of this work was done by sociologists and psychologists rather than economists. Conflict situations in several important industries— meatpacking, railroads, and longshore—led to more extensive research. The Armour Automation Committee (in meatpacking) sponsored several useful studies on the problems of relocating displaced workers, training them for new jobs, and modifying seniority and other rules. The prolonged dispute in the railroad industry over the employment of firemen-helpers on diesel locomotives led to the appointment, in 1960, of a Presidential Railroad Commission that contracted a series of academic studies on this and related issues. In connection with the longshore disputes, the government conducted detailed statistical surveys of the size of work gangs and productivity. The Bureau of Labor Statistics has also done a number of interesting case studies of adjustment to technological change.

A major stimulus to research on technological change since 1962 has been the U.S. Labor Department's Office of Manpower Policy, Evaluation, and Research, originally called the Office of Manpower, Automation, and Training. Among the many projects that it contracted to university researchers was a study of management decisions to automate in gray-iron foundries at various levels of technology and a study to develop a methodology for measuring and predicting the impact of technological changes on employment and occupations.

In 1966, the National Commission on Technology, Automation, and Economic Progress, appointed by President Johnson to review the long-run implications of rapid technological change, issued the most elaborate report on the subject since the publications of the Temporary National Economic Committee of the Congress in the late 1930's.[20] Buttressed by an elaborate set of monographs by social scientists from the government, universities, and independent consulting agencies, the commission concluded that technological change had accelerated since 1947 in comparison with the preceding thirty-six years, but that the rate of increase did not have any alarming implications for the maintenance of full employment. The commission recommended that to facilitate adjustment to change, educational opportunities should be extended, a national computerized job-man matching system should be established, the government should become "an employer of last resort, providing work for the 'hard-core unemployed' in useful community enterprises," and "serious study" should be given to a "minimum income allowance" or "negative income tax program." Although not likely to be fully implemented immediately, the report reflected the substantial progress that research into the problems of the labor market had achieved. On the other hand, it also pointed out many gaps in knowledge, as reflected in the conclusion that new means must be discovered of "making our institutions flexible and adaptable while maintaining the mechanisms of free choice and democratic participation."

Organizational Behavior and Interpersonal Relations

Some of the most fruitful advances in recent labor relations research have emerged out of the study of the internal organizations of management and labor. The postwar "behavioral science" (a term popularized in the McCarthy period when "social science" seemed to be confused with "socialism" by some Congressmen) and its new brand of "organization theory" have, to some degree, superseded the old institutionalism, although the developers have been mainly sociologists and psychologists rather than economists, and industrial organizations are only one of their interests. Many of these scholars identify themselves as behavioral scientists just as the earlier (and some contemporary) scholars considered themselves institutionalists.

One of the main sources of the new approach was the work of Elton Mayo and his Harvard Business School associates in the 1920's and 1930's, particularly as reflected in the Western Electric Hawthorne experiments. Mayo was principally concerned with the training of administrators and managers in the art of achieving "spontaneous collaboration," or teamwork, in the enterprise. His ideas about leadership, especially when taken in conjunction with the writings of Chester Barnard, gave a major stimulus to organizational research from the perspective of the administrator. His insights into the nature of informal work groups as an element in shaping worker morale and behavior similarly stimulated a host of studies.

The second main source of postwar organizational studies was the surveys by industrial psychologists like Arthur Kornhauser and J. David Houser into the attitudes of workers toward their jobs and their employers. These scholars contended that the study of activities was not sufficient to an understanding of the process of social change and that an understanding of the perceptions, motivations, and evaluations of individuals, systematically gathered, was essential. The development of statistical sampling techniques, in large measure derived from the biometricians, was a timely aid to this approach.

For about a decade and a half after the end of World War II, human relations research flourished, resulting in a notable increase in knowledge about employer-employee communications, attitudes and "attitudinal climates," and relations among workers and between workers and supervisors at the shop or office level. The plant was viewed as a small society, the culture of which could be studied as sociologists and anthropologists studied other types of societies. Although Mayo was severely criticized by C. Wright Mills and others for being pro-management and for seeking to manipulate workers to serve managerial ends, his influence was reflected in such widely read studies as George C. Homans' *The Human Group,* in which Homans introduced his interactionist concepts of sentiments, symbols, and activities; W. Lloyd Warner and J. O. Low's Yankee City volume on *The Social System of a Modern Factory;* and Benjamin Selekman's *Labor Relations and Human Relations.* In turn, Warner and Homans deeply influenced William F. Whyte who, together with his students at the University of Chicago and Cornell University, became the most productive researcher in industrial human relations and plant cultures. Whyte's studies in the areas of communication channels and wage payments as production incentives have been especially enlightening. Closely rivaling the Whyte team's research products were the studies of Yale's Charles R. Walker and Robert Guest of the impact of technology and technological change on factory workers' attitudes.

Another early leader in the postwar study of organizations was E. Wight Bakke, also of Yale University. Bakke attempted to construct a dynamic model of organizations in which "four basic resources: people, materials, ideas, and nature," are welded together for the purpose of solving problems related to the purpose of the organization. He has been particularly interested in the "organizational charter" and the "fusion process" between an organization and the individuals comprising it.[21] Bakke's concepts have been elaborated and tested by Chris Argyris, who has explored the regions of conflict between the goals of the organization and the individual.

Douglas McGregor, a social psychologist at MIT, was less concerned with organizational structure; his focus was on the way management directed and controlled the human resources of the organization.[22] He concluded from recent scientific findings about human motivation that the traditional view that people dislike work and need to be coerced or manipulated was in error. Instead, he held that the key to successful management was the imaginative integration of individual and organizational goals and the creation of an organizational climate conducive to the development and "self-actualization" of the individual, with an emphasis on working together. McGregor's theorizing owed much to the writings of A. H. Maslow. He found a practical model in the Scanlon Plan, the creation of his colleague Joseph Scanlon, an ex-unionist, who was concerned with the promotion of union-management cooperation and industrial efficiency through a suggestion system combined with a plant-wide bonus based on the sharing of efficiency gains. The Scanlon Plan itself has been adopted in only a small number of enterprises, although McGregor's work has reached a large audience in the universities and industry.

Peter Drucker examined the organization and decision-making process of a corporation from the standpoint of its key role in modern industrialized society. To him, the economic functions and the technological characteristics of the corporation were more fundamental than interpersonal relations. His "new society" envisioned an institutional structure in which workers were given a high degree of participation in the non-economic aspects of the corporation, but in which the management retained a strong responsibility for the economic performance of the organization.[23]

In contrast to the focus on formal organization of writers like Drucker and Bakke, Melville Dalton approached organizational behavior through the role of participant observer studying the informal interactions of managers and subordinates. Dalton's major work challenged traditional bureaucratic theory by showing that conflict was inherent in organizational life and had positive as well as negative effects, and that there is often a wide gap between official and unofficial behavior and between formal and informal groupings. He pointed out that a great deal of behavior is masked to conform ostensibly to rules and formal roles but, in fact, deviates sharply from them, and that a continual struggle goes on between impersonal organization and the personalizing individual.[24] He also was one of the first researchers to emphasize lateral relationships among managers (both staff and line) as distinct from the conventional focus on superior-subordinate relations.

The University of Michigan's Institute for Social

Research, under the leadership of Rensis Likert, has contributed to the understanding of industrial organizations from two directions. Its Survey Research Center has been in the forefront of those researchers utilizing sample survey interviews and questionnaires in the study of worker attitudes, supervisory styles, and worker productivity. A ten-year research project on the interrelationships of these three variables suggests that worker morale is a multidimensional phenomenon, not to be summed up in a single factor, and that high or low productivity does not bear a simple, direct relationship to any one style of supervision. The Research Center for Group Dynamics, the Institute's other main research arm, concentrated on small group behavior, its most interesting studies on labor problems indicating that a more democratic, participative approach is more likely to facilitate the introduction of new processes or techniques than an authoritarian approach. Likert, like McGregor, has made participation a major variable in his approach.

The interests of the Survey Research Center and the Research Center for Group Dynamics converged in a major five-year study of organizational stress, with particular attention to role conflict and ambiguity. One result of the study is a new role theory of organizational structure that diverged not only from the more conventional views, but also from Likert's theory, which was derived from the earlier work of the Michigan Institute.[25] The organization is seen as "an array of overlapping role sets" in which the key dynamic element is role expectations. The communication of role expectations "begins the basic cycle by which organizational performance is insured" and at the same time creates the widespread conditions of role conflict and ambiguity.

The studies of the Michigan Institute on work attitudes and performance represent only a small part of the research in this area. Victor H. Vroom cites over 500 investigations in his 1964 survey.[26] He concluded that certain generalizations can be supported by evidence from various of these researches (e.g., that job satisfaction is directly related to the extent to which jobs provide outcomes that people desire to attain, and that occupational choices can be predicted from measures of the strength of people's values or motives). On the other hand, in many aspects of the subject, evidence was limited or conflicting (e.g., there was little evidence for predicting or accounting for the influence of sex or of father's occupation on occupational choice; likewise the interrelations of participation in decision-making, knowledge of results, and work satisfaction were not clearly determined). Vroom also noted that his focus on motivation in work had consciously excluded the equally important psychological relations to work of learning, perception, and problem-solving. Sociologists could have added, with equal justice, such factors as reference group attachment, the social prestige of jobs, and class differentiation or social stratification.

The subject of leadership has vied with attitudes as a prime research topic for industrial and social psychologists. At Ohio State University, Carroll L. Shartle, Ralph M. Stogdill, and John K. Hemphill were among the first to stress the significance of situational factors, as well as traits, in accounting for leadership differences. At Illinois, Fred E. Fiedler has conducted extensive research into leadership and group effectiveness that indicates that leader acceptance by the group is a particularly important variable, with the power of the leader's position and the structure of the task performed by the group as of lesser importance. These and other studies have shown the need for increasingly complex and sophisticated approaches.[27]

Many of the psychologists, political scientists, and sociologists who have been studying and theorizing about organizational life have, of course, not been primarily concerned with labor relations. Among these the names of Herbert Simon, James G. March, Alvin Gouldner, and Peter M. Blau are prominent illustrations. By and large, they have been interested in the decision-making process from the view of the administrator or in the structure and functioning of bureaucracies as social institutions. The labor field is heavily indebted to such scholars.[28]

Although the primary emphasis of organization students has been on the corporation and the relations between management and employees, the trade union as an institution has not been neglected. It may be recalled that some of the most distinguished early writings—by the Johns Hopkins group and by Hoxie at Chicago—dealt with this subject. However, the studies between the two world wars of trade union organization and policy failed to break new ground. Many of the post-World War II works, like the Trade Union Monograph Series of the Center for the Study of Democratic Institutions and Harvard University's Studies in Labor-Management History, were also in the traditional style, largely stressing formal organization and procedures and historical evolution.

The newer approach of the sociologists and psychologists, as well as of some institutional economists, on the other hand, included a concern with informal group behavior, the attitude of members and leaders, channels of communication, and role conflicts. Leonard R. Sayles and George Strauss, under the influence of

William F. Whyte, were among the first to throw a powerful spotlight on the human relations within the local union—the personal as well as group pressures bearing on the shop stewards and the union officers, the conflict of interest groups in the organization, and the interaction of formal and informal procedures. In later studies, they enlarged on these elements, showing how they were shaped by technological and other elements of the plant environment.[29] Joel Seidman and his associates at the University of Chicago, relying on extensive interviews with workers and leaders as well as on personal observations, were able to develop an interesting typology of union members ranging from the ideological unionist to the indifferent member and the unwilling unionist. Bernard Karsh, then a Seidman associate, used the same approach to portray the evolution of an organizing strike in a small Wisconsin plant. A number of valuable surveys of union membership attitudes toward the union and its leaders were conducted, including those by Hjalmar and R. A. Hudson Rosen (in metal working), Theodore Purcell (in meat packing), and the Illini City group (in five different industrial situations). Among the findings of these and related studies were the independent views of the members on union political action and support for the dual loyalty thesis that pro-union men tended also to have favorable views about the employer, while union critics also tended to be unfavorable to management.

As in the case of the corporations, a variety of scholars have been interested in union leadership, from the level of the shop steward to the presidency of the international union. A comprehensive review of union leadership studies by Lois Macdonald in 1958 elicited some favorable comments but in general indi-

cated the need for more analytical and realistic research.[30] Since then the field has been enriched by
Sidney M. Peck's intimate participative observation
study of local shop leaders in Milwaukee and by
Ralph and Estelle James' revealing portrayal of Hoffa
as president of the Teamsters Union, as well as the
series sponsored by the Center for the Study of Democratic Institutions. Obviously, however, much more
work remains to be done in this area.

Unfortunately, the new approach has not yet been
widely incorporated in the study of international
unions. A few important exceptions, however, illus-
trate the possibilities: namely, C. Wright Mills' survey
of the personal characteristics of national union leaders,
Harold L. Wilensky's analysis of intellectual staff
members of unions, the Seymour M. Lipset and associates' study of the International Typographical
Union, and the James' examination of Hoffa's leadership of the Teamsters Union.

Another important development of the past decade has been the revival of interest in the subject
of union democracy. The stimulus for this revival
appears to have come from a number of different
sources—the emergence of the union movement as
part of the big business, big labor, big government
trinity; widespread journalistic interest in the "organization man" and individual freedom in a mass
society; the abuses revealed by the U.S. Senate's
McClellan Committee; and the revitalization of social
and political theories of bureaucracy. The Lipset-
Trow-Coleman study of the internal politics of the
ITU is an outstanding work in this area not only
because of the quality of the research but also because
of its theoretical framework and conclusions. In brief,
this study found the ITU to be an exception to the

"iron law of oligarchy" propounded by the German sociologist Robert Michels,[31] which maintains that large-scale organization "gives birth to the domination" of the leaders over the followers, and that oligarchy is a more natural form than democracy in organizational life.

Subsequent studies by, for example, Arnold S. Tannenbaum and Robert L. Kahn of the University of Michigan and Alice Cook of Cornell have demonstrated a wide variety of patterns at the local union level ranging from highly democratic to highly authoritarian. Tannenbaum and Kahn suggest "that we should think less in terms of the autocratic-democratic dichotomy and more in terms of the basic dimensions of control, within which an infinite number of patterns can be found."[32] But this judgment, which has considerable merit in operational terms, has not been generally accepted because democracy symbolizes more than control, and union democracy involves a set of values that must be confronted rather than bypassed.

Foreign Labor and International Comparisons

Prior to World War II, American students of labor economics and labor relations showed relatively little serious interest in research abroad, although the U.S. Bureau of Labor Statistics had from its beginning shown a continual interest in foreign experience with respect to old-age pensions, unemployment insurance, health insurance, employment services, and the like. Selig Perlman's *Theory of the Labor Movement* compared Russian, British, and German experience with the American, but it relied mainly on the author's personal experience as a youth, on documents, and on the research of others. Only a few scholars conducted first-hand studies abroad (e.g., Lewis L. Lorwin on the international labor movement, David J. Saposs on French labor, and Carter L. Goodrich on British labor's participation in management). After World War II, however, there was an explosion of interest in foreign labor, due partly to America's new role in the world and partly to availability of funds for such research. One of the most ambitious undertakings was the Kerr-Dunlop-Harbison-Myers interuniversity study of Labor Problems in Economic Development, with its focus on the responses of managers, labor, and government to industrialization in contrast to earlier foci on the labor movement and capitalism.[33] Like the earlier work, however, this project was institutionally oriented, unrelated to orthodox economic growth theory. It has been succeeded by a comprehensive investigation of the relationships between education and industrialization in newly developing economies.

Numerous other scholars have extended foreign research to almost every major sector of the labor and industrial relations field. One of the most fruitful subjects of study has been that of worker and union participation in management. Studies have been made of German codetermination, British joint consultation, the Yugoslav and Polish workers councils, and the joint production committees in Israel. Because Americans have had relatively little experience with these types of organizational devices (the major exception being the joint production committees of World War II), the foreign studies serve as interesting subjects for comparative analysis. This is equally applicable to studies of European and Australian dispute settlement procedures, such as the labor courts, and of industry-wide and national collective bargaining systems which have been developed on a much more extensive and diversified scale than in this country. A study by W. H. McPherson and Frederic Meyers of the French labor court system suggests a number of ideas to Americans concerned with dispute settlement.

Knowledge about strikes has also advanced appreciably, not only as to their volume and intensity, but also as to their industrial and occupational characteristics. Clark Kerr and Abraham Siegel, in a study of eleven countries, have shown that certain industries are much more strike prone than others and have hypothesized that, at least for the most extreme cases, the tendency of the industrial environment to direct workers into isolated masses is a major causal factor. Arthur Ross and his colleagues pursued international strike comparisons more intensively and endeavored to explain the existence of a number of country patterns and, in particular, to account for the "withering away of the strike" in most of the countries of northern Europe. Recent experience indicates that the strike, even in these countries, remains an important economic weapon.

Studies of national strike experience have had to rely heavily, for analytical purposes, on studies of national industrial relations systems, labor movements, and managerial ideologies. Volumes containing essays by specialists on various countries have been edited by Walter Galenson (on labor movements and economic development) and by Adolf Sturmthal (on collective bargaining and white-collar unionism). Among the numerous one-man studies, mention may be made of the research in western Europe by Sturmthal, in Scandinavia by Galenson, in Japan by Solomon B. Levine, in France by Val R. Lorwin, in Israel by

Irvin Sobel and this author, in Italy by Daniel Horowitz and Maurice F. Neufeld, in India by Charles A. Myers, and in Latin America by Robert J. Alexander. Studies of the labor movement and collective relations, while introducing new data and new ideas, were for the most part plowing old fields. Reinhard Bendix's historical exploration of management ideologies in England, Russia, and the United States tilled virgin territory.

In the wages and incomes policy areas, there was also significant research of a comparative nature. The Reynolds-Taft analysis of wage structures has already been noted. Similar work was done by Melvin Rothbaum, who made an exhaustive survey of published sources and spent a year in Europe searching for primary material. An interesting statistical analysis of foreign (mostly European) and American data on changes in wages, prices, production, and unemployment for the decade ending in 1962 was done by Joseph W. Garbarino as a basis for assessing national income policy and income behavior. Also quite recently, Murray Edelman and R. W. Fleming, from the perspectives of a political scientist and a lawyer, conducted a study of national incomes policy in Britain, the Netherlands, Italy, and Germany assessing the effectiveness of governmental behavior in this field.[34]

This research into foreign experience, despite its volume, has barely scratched the potential territory. It has, however, had profound impact on the work of American and foreign scholars. For one thing, it has greatly broadened the conceptual schemes being used. American practices have been subjected to new standards, and ideas that have not yet been tested in America have been introduced. New questions are being asked. The exportability of American industrial

relations, accepted too readily in many lands immediately after World War II, has been subjected to
serious challenge. The comparative method, as a mode
of research, has been refined and elaborated although
many of the studies have been technically crude and
unimpressive. Value premises and judgments in research have been given a new emphasis.

Industrial Society

In his introduction to a collection of readings that
he entitled *The Classic Tradition*, C. Wright Mills
called attention to the importance of looking at society as a whole (at its main drift) and of constructing
models of society that provide a general orientation
as well as a basis for developing specific theories and
hypotheses. The nineteenth and early twentieth cen-
turies were the time of the grand theorizers—Comte,
Fourier, Marx, Proudhon, Spencer, Freud, Durkheim,
and Weber, to cite some of the most important. Almost
all of them were Europeans. Except for a few utopians
like Edward Bellamy, the pragmatically oriented
Americans of the nineteenth century were not attuned
to constructing grand designs of society, even though
they borrowed ideas liberally from the Europeans. The
major twentieth-century exception was Thorstein
Veblen, who, until relatively recently, was regarded
as an "outsider" rather than as a forerunner of things
to come. Among the scholars in the United States
specializing in labor and industry, Mayo's conception
of the established and adaptive societies was something
of a rarity and was largely dependent, as he forth-
rightly stated, on the ideas of a Frenchman, Emile
Durkheim, and an Italian, Vilfredo Pareto. Mayo, it
should be noted, was an Australian by birth and train-

ing and had worked in England before coming to the United States as a mature scholar.

In the first decade or so after World War II, sociologists with an interest in labor tended to focus on the culture of the plant society, as has been seen; but then plant human relations seemed to lose its attraction as a research topic for many, and interest shifted to the wider culture, as reflected in the work of Reinhard Bendix on management ideologies in the course of industrialization, the writings of Bendix and Seymour Lipset on social mobility, and a considerable literature on social conflict. Some labor specialists, as well as a number of scholars to whom labor is a subordinate area of interest, turned their attention to the fundamental nature and drift of industrial society— partly, perhaps, because of concerns about the future of American society, and partly because of America's new role in world affairs. Several different approaches may be identified. There are the scholars who are interested in the alienating forces and values in a technological, competitive society, like Erich Fromm, Robert Blauner, and Robert Presthus; the policy-oriented students of economic development in industrializing nations, like the Kerr-Dunlop-Myers-Harbison team; and the social critics who fear the job-destroying impact and social maladjustments of automation and rapid technological change, like Robert Theobald, Michael Harrington, and Ben Seligman.

Borrowing again from C. Wright Mills on "the classic tradition," one might transfer to the new social theorists his observation that

it is not only the scope and the interrelations of their questions and the fact that they are "soaked in history" that define the classical workmen. It is also the fact that their intellectual problems are relevant to the public issues of their times and to the private troubles of individual men and women. More than that—they have helped to define more clearly the issues and the troubles and the intimate relations between the two.[35]

Conclusions

Even from this brief and sketchy survey, it is apparent that research in the labor field has progressed during the postwar period. But this progress has been very uneven among the different subdivisions of the field, and innumerable challenging problems remain to be explored. What may be said in conclusion?

Although useful research has continued in all of the major sections of the field, the emphasis has shifted from the traditional areas of labor history, union-management relations, and labor law to the newer problems of manpower policy and income security, organizational behavior, the nature of work and technology, and economic development. These shifts have not occurred because the earlier problems have been exhausted, but rather because important new problems have emerged, and public interest and public funds have moved in these new directions. For better or worse, research has tended to shift with the "headlines."

Also, the scope of the field has widened. During the time when union organization was a conflict issue and collective bargaining was limited to a small sector of the economy, research focused on unionization and related problems. Now that collective bargaining has been firmly institutionalized in the blue-collar industries, and the interests of the labor movement have been directed beyond the job to virtually all aspects of national life, students of labor have, in effect, followed along. The growth of government involvement in labor affairs has had a similar influential effect.

Third, with the expansion of research has come an intensification, or deepening, of investigations. More subtle and sophisticated questions are being asked about internal processes and environmental pressures. In part, at least, this is due to the involvement of other disciplines besides economics and law. Sociologists have probed into informal as well as formal procedures and practices; psychologists have explored motivations as well as evaluations; political scientists have searched the processes of public policy formation, not merely the end product. Institutionalists have been concerned with the differential effects of environmental factors and not merely with a listing of them.

Finally, as a result of a growing interest in the development of theoretical models and general principles, sensitivity to the limitations of knowledge has increased. In every subdivision of the field, important gaps have been identified. In history, for example, there is a need for more knowledge of the unskilled laboring class and of the unorganized. Why have the unorganized been deterred from joining a patently successful labor movement? In the union-management sphere, the handling of public employee strikes is a major challenge. In the public policy area, evaluations of the consequences of legislation, administrative agency actions, and court decisions have been few and far between. Even less of an evaluative nature has been achieved in the private sectors. In the organizational behavior area, the prediction of successful leadership remains unresolved. Employee participation in decision-making continues to be a controversial and ambiguous problem. How best to help the poor through attacks on structural unemployment (training, education, mobility aids, and antidiscrimination activities) is one of many labor market issues calling for research. On the international scene, the question of the extent to which American labor policies and practices can be transferred to the newer industrializing nations is worth further study. And the overall character of mass industrialized society poses the serious problem of how man can maintain his individuality and creativity in the face of powerful alienating technological and bureaucratic forces. These are only a few illustrative questions of the many calling for research in the various branches of the field.

Methodological Problems

Researchers in labor problems have relied heavily on the ideas and techniques of the various social sciences —economics, sociology, anthropology, psychology, political science, and history—as well as of the languages of science—mathematics, statistics, and logic. Like other social scientists, they have also been influenced by the methodologies of the more successful physical and biological disciplines, although neither the axiomatic approach nor the experimental methods of these disciplines have been widely imitated. By and large, labor researchers have been borrowers of methodology rather than innovators.

In this treatment of research methodology, attention is directed to each of the major phases of the research process as well as to certain questions that are of a more general nature. Thus, the first four sections deal with problem formulation, study design, data collection techniques, and data analysis and interpretation. The subsequent three sections consider the role of values, disciplinary versus interdisciplinary approaches, and individual versus team research. The Appendix, moreover, presents an outline of a course for advanced undergraduate and first-year graduate students on research in labor as a systematic guide to training in the contemporary scene.

Problem Formulation

Problem formulation encompasses the all-important initial phases of research in which a problematic situation is reduced to what John Dewey terms the relevant factual situation. In this process, the key variables or concepts are identified and operationally defined, the underlying assumptions and value premises are made explicit, and the direction of the search for the relevant facts is determined. Only two aspects of problem formulation will be treated here—the use of concepts and the role of theory. In both cases, the literature reveals serious limitations and the need for critical reconsideration.

In a session of the 1965 annual meeting of the Industrial Relations Research Association devoted to concept analysis in industrial relations, the author noted that the vitality and significance of any scientific field of knowledge depend in large measure on the key concepts around which scholars determine and direct their research.[1]

The concepts that have been most important to the advancement of the labor field fall into two categories: those developed by social scientists for their respective disciplines and those developed by specialists in labor problems. Examples of the first are the economist's concepts of the labor market and productivity, the sociologist's concepts of class and alienation, and the psychologist's concepts of morale and satisfaction. Examples of the second kind are collective bargaining, the appropriate bargaining unit, union democracy, and job security.

Adequate conceptualization must meet three tests:

1. Relevancy—Does the idea expressed in a concept relate in a meaningful way to important problems in the field? Is the concept likely to be a fruitful source of hypotheses and key questions for the solution or illumination of a problem?

2. Definitional clarity—Is the concept defined with sufficient clarity and precision so that its meaning is understood by its users?

3. Operationalism—Is the concept defined in such a way as to permit it to be studied empirically?

As one examines the main concepts of the research literature in relation to the three tests, the concepts that have been developed by specialists in labor problems seem to be particularly vulnerable to criticism. Many are ambiguous. The same term often gains very different meanings over time. Each researcher tends to develop his own definition instead of building on the work of his predecessors. Standardization, which is so vital to development of scientific knowledge, is conspicuously absent in many branches of the field.

Take, for instance, the concept of management rights or management prerogatives, which became a highly controversial issue during World War II and was the chief stumbling block to agreement in President Truman's postwar Labor-Management Conference of 1945. Neil Chamberlain, who has written about this subject as much as anybody, notes that most students and practitioners have treated this concept in decision-making terms and have envisioned unions, for better or worse, as invaders of managerial authority in the decision-making process. He then identifies four different interpretations of this concept. However, he himself rejects the concept of management as the primary decision-maker and argues instead for a concept in which management *coordinates* the bargaining among the various interest groups in the enterprise concerned with particular problems or decisions and which thereby maintains the organizational integrity of the enterprise.[2] In a somewhat related way, Margaret Chandler proposes to discard the property-based rights concept in favor of one based on organizational process —"to move from management as a keeper of property to management as a promoter of process."[3]

Myron Joseph has subjected an even more fundamental concept—bargaining—to a similar analysis. He notes that bargaining is invariably used in relation to some other word, such as collective bargaining, bargaining power, or bargaining relationship. He then distinguishes and analyzes a series of different interpretations of the bargaining concept that appear in the literature. Included are L. Reed Tripp's view of bargaining as a relationship between socioeconomic groups in an economy with social and political dimensions; Joseph Shister's definition as the total pattern of relationships between organized labor and management within the institutional framework of the society of the United States; Neil Chamberlain's three-fold conceptualization of bargaining as an exchange relationship for the purpose of selling labor, a constitutional system in industry, and a method of business management; H. Gregg Lewis' view of a union-management decision process with a primary focus on interorganizational relationships; and Robert E. Walton and Robert B. McKersie's concept of bargaining as an interaction process. Joseph then points out how these various concepts have been used by their adherents to explore different types of problems and to exploit different kinds of research methódology.

His concluding paragraph warrants quoting:

In spite of the fact that bargaining has been conceptualized in many different ways, some of which I have found to be relatively sterile, it remains a key concept—or more accurately, represents several key concepts—in the field of industrial relations. The bargaining concept has shown vitality in that it continues to be redefined so that it can provide an effective base for a variety of different kinds of research. I believe it would be a mistake to try to force the structure back into one grand concept, although every effort should be made to explore the interfaces among the different interpretations of bargaining, and to build them together where that can be done meaningfully.[4]

The importance and problems of conceptualization have been discussed by other scholars. Valuable examples are to be found in Murray Edelman's analysis of the concept of power, Daniel Bell's discussion on work, Hiram S. Davis' treatment of productivity, and Herbert Parnes' comments on labor force concepts. Although these and other writings reveal a clear recognition of the role of conceptualization in research, this understanding has often not been reflected in research reports.

Another aspect of problem formulation that has been inadequately treated in the labor research field has been the role of theory and hypothesis. The textbook model of the research process in which theory plays a major part in identifying and connecting the key variables and in suggesting hypotheses for empirical testing is applicable to only a small portion of the research actually conducted. Social science research in the United States has for many decades been fact oriented rather than theory oriented. Labor research has tended to follow a similar pattern. In both cases, however, there are notable exceptions, and these exceptions have been growing in number and significance in the last two decades.

The heavy emphasis on purely empirical research, that is, on research which seeks to obtain answers to one or more key questions of a descriptive, diagnostic, or predictive nature, stems from two main beliefs. One is that labor relations is a practical art, not a science, and, therefore, generalization is neither feasible nor helpful in coping with its concrete policy or decision problems. If there are relevant scientific principles, they are the responsibility of scholars in the more basic disciplines. The other belief is that the subject is so complex and knowledge of it is so incomplete that it is premature to theorize.

It might be supposed that the industrial psychologists would be more theory oriented than other academicians in the field. But this is not the case. In his address as president of the division of industrial psychology of the American Psychological Association, Brent Baxter observed:

The paucity of theoretical formulations when working on industrial problems is leading us in several unfortunate directions. My plea is to increase the development of theory and to make use of it as a focal point for research, for applications, and for problem solving.[5]

In developing his argument, Baxter noted: "Our prediction of the behavior of employees, management, or unions has increased relatively little in the last ten or twenty years. The rapidly growing number of articles in industrial psychology does not reflect fundamental advances but more often a multiplicity of minor tinkerings in a wide variety of settings." And at another point he asserted:

With our lack of emphasis on a fundamental and broad psychological approach we have drifted towards becoming technicians and not scientists. Our orientation is toward methodology and techniques. If management has a selection problem, we can build a test. If there's a development problem, we know how to build a rating scale. If morale is shaky, we can develop an opinion survey. We are better known for our techniques than for fundamental insights.

It is not uncommon to find hypotheses being used as research guides without any relation to a broader theoretical framework. Sometimes these hypotheses are the conclusions of prior studies; at others they are simply the hunches of the researcher based on personal experience or observation. Hypotheses of this more or less isolated character do not differ from key questions. Their limitation is that they do not relate the research to more fundamental assumptions or propositions. They are useful because they identify the relevant variables and often suggest important connections or relationships among them. Thus they give the research a positive thrust—the researcher has a searchlight and is not obliged to prowl aimlessly and blindly for the requisite data. On the other hand, the isolated hypothesis (perhaps more than the key question) carries with it the danger that the researcher will become so attached to it that he will, usually quite unconsciously, select the evidence that tends to support the hypothesis and reject the evidence that does not. The obvious solution to this problem is always to use more than one alternative hypothesis, not simply the null hypothesis or its reverse but an alternative involving one or more different variables.

Research that is linked to or derived from a more general theoretical (or conceptual) framework has been the exception rather than the rule. Nevertheless it has been a concern of a number of scholars, and there are indications that it will become more frequent. The pre-World War II literature contains several classic illustrations, such as Commons' study of the expanding areas of market competition in the case of the American shoemakers from 1648 to 1895, and Paul Douglas' testing of the marginal productivity theory of wages against American experience from 1890 to 1926.

Since 1945, theory-oriented research has been conducted along a variety of lines, of which the following illustrations warrant some discussion—studies of labor economists into the operations of the labor market and of wage structures; sociopsychological studies of intraorganizational behavior; and studies of union-management relations.

One of the few efforts in the union-management area to develop a theoretical framework that might be tested through research was John Dunlop's work on industrial relations systems. As has been seen, the Dunlop framework does not actually provide a theory about the interconnections of key variables, but rather it identifies a set of human variables interacting within a set of environmental variables to produce a network of rules for the work place and the work community. Dunlop does not explain the dynamics of the process through which particular rules emerge, but he does suggest, and provides empirical data to support, the idea that certain contexts tend to be correlated with certain rules. From his framework, it is possible to generate numerous hypotheses, the testing of which might add considerable understanding to this aspect of the labor field.

Although the Dunlop approach has been widely discussed and even utilized in the classroom, efforts to apply it empirically have not proved particularly successful to date. A similar fate has characterized other ventures. Thus, a number of scholarly enterprises that started out with a purely empirical approach have concluded with efforts at theorizing; but these resultant theories have not in turn, as yet, led to empirical tests of the theories or hypotheses deduced from them. Examples are the National Planning Association study of the causes of industrial peace, the interuniversity project on labor in economic development, and the Illini City research on labor-management relations in three Illinois communities.

In the organizational or sociopsychological area, somewhat more progress in relating theory and research has been made. Two examples may be cited. One of the most ambitious and elaborate efforts is that of E. Wight Bakke and Chris Argyris at Yale. In an interim report of 1954 they stated that their basic objective was

to contribute to the creation of an integrated theory of human behavior useful to all who are interested in interpreting, understanding, predicting, and regulating behavior within and in relation to any type of social organization. . . . On the empirical level, studies conducted since 1938 in going organizations have been directed toward developing a framework of empirically verifiable and operationally useful concepts and models necessary and adequate for the study of human behavior within and in relation to organizations.[6]

Although their theory of the "fusion process" has been developed in a number of books and articles and has reached a wide audience, it does not appear to have persuaded other scholars to adopt it as their starting point for further work.

Another theory-directed research series stems from

the theories and experiments of Kurt Lewin in the area of authoritarian versus democratic leadership. Several of Lewin's colleagues and students, including Ronald Lippitt, Dorwin Cartwright, and L. A. Festinger, have pursued these ideas in the industrial setting, especially in connection with employee participation in decisions affecting changes, and have concluded that participatory management is more effective. Despite promising results that have been accepted by other industrial and social psychologists, the empirical testing of participation theory has been so limited that firm generalization or statement of principle are not justified.

A summation of the work in organization theory, based on a seminar in the social science of organizations, notes that the subject is so complex (involving at least 200 variables "which make a difference") and research resources so limited that a major problem is what strategy to apply to the study of the subject.[7] At least eighteen different conceptualizations of groups and organizations were found:

It is often difficult to find any overlap between two different systems of variables. The systems developed by business organization theorists, behavior scientists, and operations researchers are likely to consist of widely different variables. Each developer is likely to insist that his system includes the variables that are really important to a theory of organization. The value systems and theoretical allegiances of different schools of thought tend to make each distrustful of the concepts and problems regarded as important by the others.[8]

Nonetheless, this discussion reveals that theory-related research, including some important work by students of labor, is growing, although on a fragmented basis.

In the area of labor economics, and particularly the

labor market, theory had been separated from empirical study for many decades. Economists had built up a highly rigorous theoretical model of the labor market (as well as of product markets) but, as the World War II experience in wage and manpower controls revealed, there was considerable discrepancy between the theory and reality. Immediately after the end of the War, the Social Science Research Council established a Committee on Labor Market Research to bridge the gap. As a result of the encouragement and support of this committee, a substantial number of field and statistical studies were undertaken to test hypotheses derived from current theory and to develop more sophisticated theory. Leaders in this development included Lloyd Reynolds, Charles Myers, Gladys Palmer, and Dale Yoder.

The theories and hypotheses that were subjected to empirical test were largely qualitative in character, although the research had a strong statistical flavor. Two sample hypotheses are the following, developed by Lloyd Reynolds as a result of a prior largely empirical study:

That changes in plant wage levels occur in waves—one plant raises wages when other plants are raising them. These waves are set off by forces exogenous to the firm or area, *viz.*, price and output changes in the national economy.

That differences in job opportunity can produce movement of labor even in the absence of wage differentials. The converse, however, does not hold. The mere existence of known interplant differences in wage levels is incapable of producing movement unless vacancies exist in the higher wage plants.[9]

During the past decade, largely as a result of advances in computer technology and the expansion of statistical data surveys, theory-oriented research has assumed a more precise, quantitative character. The theory of the market has been expressed in the form of models comprised of multivariable regression equations and the hypotheses have been subjected to quite elaborate statistical tests. It would be erroneous to suggest that knowledge of the labor market has been dramatically changed because of these model-guided studies, but refinements have been noticeable, and the future potential is favorable. The studies of cyclical variations in the labor supply are one example.[10] The prewar research of Wladimir S. Woytinsky had supported the hypothesis that in time of depression "additional" or "secondary" workers entered and enlarged the labor force. Clarence Long, using simple correlational analysis, challenged Woytinsky's thesis by finding a tendency for the number of "discouraged" workers who left the labor force to offset the number of additional workers. More elaborate regression analysis by Thomas F. Dernburg and Kenneth Strand, among others, suggested that while both additional and discouraged workers were concurrently involved in the labor market picture, the discouraged workers were more numerous and important. Jacob Mincer, in turn, has raised some technical questions about the various studies, and the controversy continues to flourish.

Study Design

The effective formulation of a problem is fundamental to good research, but unless the relevant data are properly gathered, the chance of obtaining the desired results is significantly reduced. This is the function of study design—a subject that has not received the attention it deserves from students of labor problems. Study design refers to the strategy and techniques of data collection; it is analogous to the architect's blueprint of a structure and the equipment used in construction. Examples are the historical case study, using both documentary and statistical data; the sample survey, using open-ended interview schedules; or the experiment, in which one group is given a particular stimulus while another carefully matched control group is not and the consequences are compared.

Different branches of the field have tended (there are, of course, numerous exceptions) to use different designs, partly because of the character of the problems and partly because of the disciplinary training of the researchers. A focus on the three subject areas discussed in the preceding section, with limited reference to some of the other areas, may facilitate the analysis.

In the labor-management area, the most common type of study design, both before and since 1945, has been the industry or establishment *case study*, relying primarily on documentary evidence (such as collective agreements, financial reports, plant and union publications, minutes of meetings, and the daily press) and semistructured interviews (using open-ended schedules or checklists of questions) with key officials and selected informants, supplemented by more or less casual personal observation. The National Planning Association's study of the causes of industrial peace is an example. Because the comprehensive case study, with its historical and evolutionary pattern, emphasizes detail and depth, it is time-consuming and expensive, and coordinated studies of a number of cases usually require the collaboration of a number of scholars, as the NPA project did. The case study is valuable as a source of insights and hypotheses but does not justify generalization, notwithstanding the tendency of some researchers to take vast leaps beyond their evidence.

When a number of case studies are conducted at about the same time, they lend themselves to the use of the *comparative method,* as Commons and associates did in a 1919 study of industrial government and as the NPA team did in the 1940's. More often, however, the comparative method is used to investigate more limited subjects than the total union-management relationship, such as grievance procedures, seniority practices, or works councils. The obvious advantage of the comparative design over the case study is that it gives more latitude to generalizing and to the testing of hypotheses, although always within specified limits. By pointing up differences as well as uniformities, comparative research helps sharpen the analytical and interpretative processes of research. It is no accident that comparative study designs are especially valuable in the international labor field where conceptual differences are so vital.

In the area of organizational structure and behavior, three different types of study design are commonly found—the sample survey, participant observation, and the controlled experiment. One of the most prominent developers of the *sample survey* is the University of Michigan's Survey Research Center under the leadership of Rensis Likert and Angus Campbell. In the labor field, the center has been particularly concerned with the relationships among three variables—worker attitudes, style of supervision, and productivity—although some of its other projects have involved worker reactions to technological change and union member participation in the activities of local unions. Sometimes all of the employees of an establishment have been studied through the administration of a so-called paper-and-pencil questionnaire; more often certain subdivisions of the establishment have been studied, with all or a sample of the employees in the subdivision covered either through written questionnaire or structured interview. The written questionnaire technique has usually been supplemented by interviews with a sample of management and union leaders.

The sample survey design owes its widespread and growing use in studies of management and labor organizations to the earlier development of mathematical sampling theory and to the practical experience of the public opinion pollsters, the census takers, and the marketing specialists. The Bureau of Labor Statistics also was early concerned with establishment sampling in its employment and wage surveys. The distinctive advantage of the sample survey is that it permits the study of and the generalization of results to large populations at a cost in time and money far smaller than that required to study a total population. The study of large numbers, of course, facilitates generalization and the testing of hypotheses. On the other hand, many of the sample surveys have sacrificed depth in favor of quantity and scope. Moreover, they have sometimes omitted important aspects that were not easy or possible to quantify. For these reasons, a number of large studies have found it advisable to combine elements of the survey and case-study designs.

The *participant observation* design is almost at the opposite end of the spectrum from the survey design. It relies on the personal experience of the researcher as a participant of the group or other unit that he is studying; it is impressionistic rather than systematic; it stresses qualitative judgment rather than quantitative summarization; and it places a heavy value on in-depth probing as against external and often superficial objectivity. Also, it yields the intensive view of the "insider" rather than the extensive scope of the "outsider" and is especially valuable in the exploration of the informal as opposed to the formal life of the organization and in the generation of hypotheses to be tested later in more systematic research. Relatively few significant participant studies by social scientists have appeared in the literature of the labor field, although many scholars have benefited intellectually from early work experiences. In the period before 1940, one of the most notable was Stanley B. Mathewson's study of the restriction of output among unorganized workers. Since 1945, the most valuable examples include Melville Dalton's perceptive analysis of informal working relations in two California plants, Donald Roy's research on the restrictive practices of work groups, Sidney Peck's study of shop stewards in a variety of Milwaukee industrial enterprises, and Harry Cohen's study of an office of the U.S. Employment Service.

Sharing many of the advantages of the participant observation approach but distinguishable from it is the research conducted on the inside by a researcher who is identified as such and makes no attempt to conceal his role. When such a researcher devotes long periods of time to an establishment, his presence ultimately becomes a natural part of the environment to the employees, and he is often able to secure a very intimate picture of the organization, although perhaps not to the same degree as the unidentified participant. This type of researcher is frequently in a position to obtain access to documents and meetings that the secret student may not. Some of the valuable research by George Strauss and Leonard R. Sayles on local unions falls in this category.

The third type of research design that sociological and psychological students of organizations have undertaken is the *field experiment*. The Western Electric Hawthorne experiments, although lacking control groups, are the best-known illustration of this design. Despite the enormous publicity given to these studies, the number of successors they have had is small. The productivity experiments under conditions of democratic and nondemocratic leadership at the Harwood sewing plant conducted by followers of Kurt Lewin in the 1940's are one outstanding example.[11] The reasons that are usually given to explain why such field experiments are uncommon are the difficulty of getting managements, unions, and employees to cooperate; the problem of obtaining control groups; and the costs entailed. Whether these reasons are valid or not, the experimentally minded behavioral scientists have tended to restrict their experiments to laboratory situations in which students have been the chief subjects and rigid controls are feasible. Thus far, there has been little carry-over from the laboratory to the labor scene.

In the labor market area, researchers, for the most part, have used one of two types of study design. One is the statistical analysis of data gathered by government agencies for general or specific purposes; the other is the use of the sample survey through written questionnaires or structured interviews. When the objective has been to gather "hard," quantitative data, the interview schedules are usually highly structured. With the increasing tendency to obtain "soft" attitudinal and motivational data as well, the interviews have ordinarily provided for some open-ended questions. In contrast to the students of organizational behavior, the labor market students have not attempted to develop new methods of data collection, but instead they have concentrated on improving their statistical concepts and techniques.

Quantification

Although the labor historians, like Ely, Commons, Norman Ware, and Selig Perlman, made little effort to compile statistical data, the state and federal bureaus of labor, under the leadership of Carroll Wright, placed a heavy emphasis on statistics, and the quantitative method has had a major part in the field from its beginning. One need only note the measurements of prices and living costs, wages and hours, accidents, work stoppages, union membership, employment and unemployment, labor turnover, and productivity. On the other hand, efforts to extend quantitative measures to other aspects of institutional behavior have been a source of some controversy in the post-World War II period.

Two positions have been taken. One argues that the more relationships and activities can be measured or otherwise quantified, the more objective and scientific the research in the field will be. Hence, efforts have been made to measure the attitudinal climate of an establishment, the extent of union influence, the morale of a work force, the degree of worker participation in the affairs of a union, the degree of bureaucratization of management, the social and economic mobility of the work force, and the interactions of supervisors and workers as well as of different levels of management. Some of these measures have been more successful than others, particularly when it has been possible to use scales with a natural number base rather than with an arbitrary zero. The arbitrary scales with unequal class intervals have been especially vulnerable to criticism. The proponents of maximum quantification have argued that even crude measurement of an ordinal (ranking) character is better than none because it improves discrimination among variables and reduces subjectivity.

The alternative position has been to support measurement when the data lend themselves to the natural number system, but to decry other efforts at quantification as superficial and misleading. Proponents of this view note that many of the most significant aspects of labor relations involve subjective feelings, values, and other intangible elements that cannot be meaningfully measured, and that imposing measurement categories and techniques on these data yields results that have the appearance of "hard" fact but are actually not a true representation. As Melville Dalton put it in a methodological exchange with the author:

The commendable aim to develop reliable methods should not become a conviction that problems must be framed solely in terms of method. This leads up the blind alley we all recognize when we *define* an attitude as a position on a scale. We have not so much defined it as we have laid out a possibly irrelevant area for exercise of our hopefully prestigeful technique. Pushed to a conclusion, operationalism makes us shy away from even recognizing a problem, unless we have techniques for dealing with it, or leads us to impose techniques that do not fit the problem. . . . I would prefer objective methods, but I doubt that exclusive use of such current devices can develop the full picture.[12]

Like so many other intellectual controversies that have occurred in the field, the difference between the disputants is one of emphasis rather than of kind. It is indisputable that some of the most important variables in the field have defied measurement. Bargaining power is one example. On the other hand, it is possible to show, historically, the notable spread and improvement of quantification and measurement as they relate to labor variables—starting with the first feeble efforts to measure objective phenomena like wages and earnings up to present-day indices of worker morale and foreman-worker interactions.

Values from a Methodological Standpoint

One of the most challenging problems confronting the labor researcher is what to do about values, for no field is more permeated with them. The term "values" includes all beliefs, opinions, standards, and norms regarding the relative desirability or worth of a thing, action, or relationship. The values of the participants strongly influence their behavior toward one another and toward the researcher. The values of the researcher affect his research in every phase from the selection of the problem to the interpretation of his data. The values of the society establish the standards by which the behavior of the participants is judged and color the environment in which they interact. Recognition of these value factors is widely reflected in the literature of the field. However, Robert M. Macdonald has effectively argued that economic analyses of the impact of unionism on wages have misfired because of "the economist's failure to surmount the ideological bias that underlies the notion of the competitive model as the *natural* order for economic relationships."[13] Murray Edelman has shown how even research that makes important contributions may "convey unintended or unwarranted normative implications."[14] A few quotations from the addresses of past presidents of the Industrial Relations Research Association may be illustrative of the pervasiveness of values:

How collective bargaining functions and what the government does in this field have important bearing upon the maintenance of a stable, high-level, and progressive economy and the preservation of democracy and individual freedom, upon which depends all else that is worth while.[15]

Industrial relations research cannot avoid value judgments. . . . The evidence collected in industrial relations research involves value judgments in the definition of terms, in the occurrence of the incident, the delimitation and classification of data, and in the determination of cause, effect, or explanation. . . . Industrial relations is not a science. Rather it is the study of the values arising in the minds, intuitions, and emotions of individuals as these values become embodied in group organization and action. The understanding and solution of problems of group organization and action can never be divorced from the more basic understanding of the values which determine individual behavior.[16]

I question whether the continuing emphasis in some quarters on promoting "free and independent" trade unions in all developing countries, presumably on the pattern of American unionism, is realistic or even helpful. The assumption is that the present American labor movement is a model for the world. But surely our labor movement is a product of the relative freedom for private interest groups in our pluralistic society as much as it is a factor contributing to this freedom. Other societies reflect different degrees of freedom for interest groups, as a consequence of economic and social factors as well as of political philosophies.[17]

It is in contributing to the study, examination and restructuring of institutions, agencies, policies, and beliefs so that they better serve our new era that the modern industrial relations researcher has his most clearly defined mandate. His task is to define and evaluate the goals and beliefs more precisely, particularly in the individual fields, to identify the forms of dysfunctionalism, to examine conflicts and identities, to spell out the alternative courses for the attainment of goals, to identify the sources of resistance to change and indicate strategies for overcoming them, to outline the progressive steps for the ultimate realization of the ends, to assist in the preparation of lists of priorities and to calculate the costs and benefits of innovations.[18]

Some social scientists have contended that the value factor should not affect the objectivity of research in social behavior. The values of the participants may be investigated like any other external phenomenon. The values of the researcher may be made explicit and discounted so as not to bias the findings. Other scholars have argued that values are so deeply imbedded in the human situation that value-free inquiry is impossible of attainment.

This view was well expressed by the editors of a volume on industrial conflict issued in 1939 by the Society for the Psychological Study of Social Issues. In justifying a position favorable to labor, the editors reported that it reflected the feelings of their members (as determined in a poll) and stated the following:

The spirit which animated the editors in organizing this Yearbook may loosely be described as scientific humanism. . . . To us this necessarily implies the liberal and progressive temper, and a repudiation of at least the worst features of the Ivory Tower tradition of what constitutes a proper intellectual life. Values are as much a part of the real world as facts; and just as facts differ in significance and weight in one's interpretation of the systems of nature, so values stand high or low in the scales of worth recognized by all individuals and all groups. Industrial conflict is meaningless except as one comprehends the antagonistic values of employers and employees. At present, no psychologist *as* psychologist can objectively demonstrate that one set of values is eventually to be preferred to another, although this is a task which he must try to solve. Decisions here are made in terms of one's ethical creed, a primitive sense of justice, the implications of democracy as a way of life in a society that is at least verbally committed to its realization, or in accordance with some congenial political pattern.[19]

In contrast, many psychologists and sociologists, closely associated with industry either as full-time employees or as consultants, did not appear to find any incompatibility between such roles and their tenet of scientific objectivity. They denied the need to take a particular position. The result in the postwar period was a rather furious debate in the professional journals and meetings over value orientations of social scientists, including the publication of a book with the contentious title *The Servants of Power.*[20]

Whichever view about values is adopted, it is clear that researchers must take a number of precautions to minimize the potentially gross biasing effect of values. First and foremost is a clear and explicit recognition that value judgments abound wherever and whenever human beings are involved. The most dangerous values are the ones that are so deeply ingrained that they are taken for granted. One of the great benefits of international comparisons, as implied in one of the preceding quotations, is that it forces the researcher to ask questions about his own concepts and assumptions and those of his subjects, something he is not likely to do when studying exclusively within his own culture. Another precaution against value bias is to explore the implications of alternative definitions, assumptions, and hypotheses for the investigation. A third is to introduce, wherever possible, multiple checks, preferably those provided by other investigators. Unfortunately, replication of studies in the same or similar contexts is the exception rather than the rule in labor research.[21]

Team and Interdisciplinary Research

The traditional image of research is that of the individual scholar pursuing his personal curiosities and exercising his personal imagination in resolving problems. As the numerous examples cited earlier in this volume indicate, this image has never accurately reflected research in the labor field. At the pioneering institutions like the University of Wisconsin and Johns Hopkins University, even Ph.D. theses in many cases were parts of team projects. There were, of course, isolated investigators who produced useful studies, but teamwork was a major element in the field. Since World War II, team projects involving two or more scholars and their assistants have probably increased relative to individual research. The reason appears to lie in the time-consuming nature of field study, which has been the primary type of study in most branches of the labor field. Even much of the documentary research has involved time-consuming field trips for the purpose of locating source material.

Thus, the question of individual versus team research has never posed a serious problem as long as the team members have had the same disciplinary backgrounds and interests. There was room for both. Shortly after World War II, however, a strong impetus was given to interdisciplinary team research by the growing interest of sociologists and psychologists in the field, by the establishment of industrial and labor relations institutes and centers—mostly on an interdisciplinary or cross-departmental staff basis—and by support and encouragement from interdisciplinary organizations like the Social Science Research Council. This approach was by no means universally applauded, although it worked with varying degrees of effectiveness in such projects as the NPA study of the causes of industrial peace, the St. Paul, Minnesota, study of employment and unemployment (carried out initially in 1940–1942 but not completed and published until 1948), the Illini City study of union-management accommodation, and the University of Chicago study of local union members.

Research that was planned and executed jointly by teams of students with different disciplinary backgrounds encompassed a much wider range of variables than was normally found in single disciplinary studies, including those of such broad-gauged institutionalists as John R. Commons. The psychologists introduced sophisticated ideas about perception, motivation, and attitude, and the sociologists provided insights about class, status, and reference groups that the labor economists had generally ignored or had treated in rather crude fashion. This enrichment of the conceptual framework was supplemented by important methodological contributions. By and large, the economists had concentrated on the techniques of documentary and statistical analysis, informal interviewing, and casual observation. The psychologists and sociologists brought with them much more refined and effective tools of field research, including structured questionnaires, attitudinal scales, projective tests, systematic observational devices, and participant observation methods. Moreover, they were more conscious of the importance of studying the informal aspects of organizational behavior, of questioning the written documents, of looking for the unintended consequences of decisions.

Interdisciplinary team research, however, also poses difficulties. Even when the team members are personally and temperamentally compatible, it takes a long time to establish a common language of communication. Unfamiliar concepts have to be explained. Diverse meanings attached to the same words have to be untangled. Even more difficult, the value premises and assumptions about man, society, and knowledge underlining the respective disciplines have to be discovered and made explicit. Although the educational values of these exchanges are often substantial, they slow down the process of planning appreciably. More serious is the fact that the team members experience considerable trouble in agreeing on their conceptual framework and methods. Students become strongly attached to particular ideas and techniques quite early in their careers, and to discard or even to compromise them often creates powerful tensions within the team. One consequence is that many concepts and methods have to be "watered down," to be treated less rigorously than the specialists are accustomed to, in order to win group consensus.

Because of these handicaps, the interdisciplinary team approach has not spread as rapidly as originally expected, and during the past decade it appears to have lost ground. Nonetheless, the nature of many of the most important problems in the labor field necessitates a breakdown of disciplinary barriers, and the fusion process has been continuing in at least two ways. One is the development of new disciplines. The other is the training of students in more than one of the traditional disciplines.

The first of these two processes is best reflected in

the area of organizational theory and analysis. Historically, the several disciplines of sociology, psychology, and political science approached the study of organizations quite separately, although there were important exceptions, as in the work of Mary Parker Follett and Harold Lasswell. The sociologists focused on organizational structure, bureaucratization, and related aspects; the psychologists were mainly interested in selection techniques, worker attitudes, supervisory styles, and conflict resolution; the political scientists concentrated on public administration. In the past two decades, each of these disciplines has broadened its scope appreciably, as reflected in the use of such labels as behavioral science, the policy sciences, operations research, and systems analysis. New professional journals have appeared, such as the *Administrative Science Quarterly, Management Science,* and *Behavioral Science,* and the joint British-American publication, *Human Relations,* which have a distinct interdisciplinary flavor. Courses taught in sociological, psychological, and political science curricula have more of an interdisciplinary focus, and graduate students in these disciplines get a broader training. Only economics has failed to follow this trend; in fact, it has tended to move in the opposite direction of narrowing its focus with the growth of mathematical model-building and econometrics.

The emergence of behavioral science has, to a degree, paralleled the old labor institutionalism in the labor field. The chief difference is that institutionalism gave primacy to economic variables whereas behavioral science emphasizes sociopsychological factors. But even the labor economists who still dominate the field (as reflected in the membership of the Industrial Relations Research Association and in the faculties of the university industrial relations centers) have been significantly influenced by behavioral science ideas and methods.

The second recent alternative to interdisciplinary team cooperation has been the training of new scholars and the retraining of older ones in the labor field to function on an interdisciplinary basis by themselves or together with others of a similar background and interest. The increasing number of graduate programs in industrial relations, both M.A. and Ph.D., which have been introduced in recent years is evidence of this development. As illustrations of the types of training offered in these programs, the course requirements for the Ph.D. at Cornell, Wisconsin, and Illinois may be cited.

At Cornell, the candidate selects a major area of specialization from one of four areas—collective bargaining, labor law and labor movements; economic and social statistics; human resources and administration; and labor economics and social security. In addition to the major area of specialization, the student ordinarily selects two minor subjects from the other areas on the list although he may choose from other fields in the graduate school as well.

At Wisconsin, three areas of concentration have been established—public policy, organizational behavior, and interpersonal behavior. The candidate may seek generalized training in all three areas, in which case he must take courses and become familiar with the methodology of at least two departments in each area. Or he may concentrate in one area—by taking courses in three departments of that area—and be prepared in one department of the other two areas as well.

At Illinois, the candidate must take three units of

research methodology (both qualitative and quantitative) applicable to the labor field, two units in industrial relations theory, and the remaining eleven units in two social science disciplines and closely related courses selected as most relevant to one of four areas of specialization—industrial relations systems and public policy; wages, labor market behavior, and income security; labor and management organizations and labor-management relations; and interpersonal and administrative behavior.

It is too early to determine the impact of such training on labor research, but it seems reasonable to predict that disciplinary lines will be much more readily crossed than where the training is wholly or almost wholly concentrated in a single discipline.

VII   *Prospects for the Future*

Developments in labor research over the past two decades may be assessed both positively and negatively. Let us see what the positive elements are.

There has been a substantial increase in the volume of research as a result of the expansion in the number of academic and governmental researchers and in the funds available for research. The emergence of some forty university institutes, schools, and centers of labor and industrial relations; the introduction of curricula leading to the M.A. and Ph.D. degrees in several of these centers; the publication of five professional journals[1] devoted exclusively to the interests of the field; and the establishment of the Industrial Relations Research Association have been particularly noteworthy features.

Also, the federal government, especially the U.S. Labor Department, has not only expanded and broadened its own research activities, but has provided large sums of money, on a contract basis, to academic researchers. In thus emulating the relationship between the defense, space, and public health agencies and the physical and life sciences, the government has given an important stimulus to labor research. The Labor Department's own fact-finding programs have vastly enriched the field, and the recent decision to increase analytical and interpretative reporting promises to enhance the value of its work.

Moreover, the involvement of sociologists, psychologists, and political scientists has added new dimensions to research in labor problems. Although the institutional economists who long dominated the field had broad social science interests and perspectives, they lacked the sophistication in certain concepts and techniques that specialists in the noneconomic social sciences developed. This was particularly true of research into the informal processes of small groups and interpersonal behavior, of studies of the attitudes, motives, and aspirations of workers and managers, of controlled experiments in factories as well as in academic laboratories, and of systematic sample surveys using interviews or questionnaires.

Finally, the subject matter of the field has deepened in emphasis and widened in scope, partly because of the injection of new scholarly interests and views, but mainly because of changes in domestic labor relations and American participation in world affairs. The internal affairs of corporate and union organizations, the technical aspects (such as fringe benefits) of established union-management relations, the employment problems of Negroes and other minority groups, retraining and other structural unemployment remedies, adaptation to technological change—these and still other topics have been investigated in much greater depth than previously and have replaced in importance the earlier concerns with the right to unionize, social security and protective labor legislation, and union history. Research in foreign countries for purpose of international comparison or as an aid to the economic development of underdeveloped countries has become a major activity.

These advances in labor research are significant, but they have been accompanied by negative elements that have hampered the growth of the field.

One such negative element is that there remains considerable ambivalence as to how best to interrelate the several social sciences in the field. One view is to emphasize each discipline as a separate entity and to encourage the study of problems that are most susceptible to attack by a particular discipline. Another is to encourage interdisciplinary cooperation in joint attacks on problems that clearly do not lend themselves to unidisciplinary solution. A third view, mindful of the difficulties of interdisciplinary cooperation in research, proposes the interdisciplinary training of scholars who can focus in an integrated way upon those problems that the disciplinary specialist cannot handle by himself.

Another problem is that labor research has tended to "follow the headlines" to an excessive degree, a tendency that has been characteristic of most of the social sciences. Unfortunately, much of such research comes too late to deal with the public problem at hand, and the underlying theoretical foundation is not adequate to support it. Just as the scholar must avoid falling into a narrow rut by unduly long and precise specialization, so he must have sufficient time, background knowledge, and technical tools to treat current problems adequately.

The "follow the headlines" phenomenon has been, to a considerable degree, a product of the large amount of money provided for research by private foundations and the federal government. It is understandable that the widespread availability of such funds attracts many individuals and institutions, but it has often led to superficial and useless research. In part, the responsibility lies with the donor organizations which, in many cases, have not formulated clearly the questions on which they seek the aid of researchers for policy-making purposes. In part, of course, it lies with the researchers themselves.

Also, the linkage of theory and research has been tenuous and limited. With some important exceptions, research in labor problems has been purely empirical, and such theory as has existed has rarely been subjected to empirical test. As a result, the field has not experienced what a physical scientist has called serial development. Instead of building on the work of predecessors, most researchers have, in effect, started from scratch. Empiricism unrelated to an explicit theoretical framework tends to encourage parallel rather than serial development in a field. Scholars find it difficult to challenge the findings of their competitors because their research is neither being replicated nor expressed in the same operational terms.

Lastly, although the involvement of the federal government in research has increased, corporate and union research on labor problems has remained disappointingly slight. A small number of large companies are conducting significant employee relations research through their own professional staffs or by contracting with academic or consulting organizations, but little of this research gets into the professional literature. Union research is mainly of a service nature to the officers of the organization. Both of these groups have the economic resources and are in highly favorable positions to undertake serious research relating to their organizations. Their failure to take advantage of the situation is unfortunate.

A look into the future in the light of this assessment of the contemporary state of the field suggests the desirability of a number of developments that leaders in the field may be able to encourage or initiate. These developments may be treated under five headings: problems warranting intensive study; concepts and theories; the impact of the computer; training for research; and relations between the academicians and the practitioners—government, corporations, unions.

Future Problems

The research of the past has been largely inspired by three motives—social reform, administrative improvement, and the development of a science. The same stimulants will exist in the future. One need not be a prophet to observe at least some of the areas of reform to which research might make a valuable contribution, since the problems have already been identified and are the subject of current research. For example, there is the great challenge of educating and training large numbers of Negro citizens so that they can be raised to a parity with the white population as members of the labor force. Another deprived sector of the economy, which includes many Negroes but is predominantly white, is composed of the migrant farm workers whose periodic efforts at organization have thus far proved largely unsuccessful and whose standards of living are shamefully low. The employment conditions of hospital and other institutional workers are also backward relative to the bulk of the population, so that reform of social standards is clearly called for.

Another level of reform, quite distinct from the problems of the poor and the discriminated, is concerned with an old but unresolved issue—the rights of public employees to form organizations and to exercise pressure to protect and further their interests. Research may be helpful in determining the conditions under which the strike is a legitimate act and in justifying alternative procedures for rule-making when the strike is banned. Since the number of public employees is steadily increasing, and the functions of government are becoming more diversified (paralleling private enterprise in many areas), these questions can be expected to become more urgent as well as more difficult to solve. The situation of the mounting number of employees of private nonprofit organizations poses a similar challenge.

A look at the more distant future indicates the need for more profound social change as a result of the far-reaching technological changes that the American economy will continue to undergo. Whether the rate of change is as rapid and dislocating as some fear or more gradual, as the President's Commission on Technology, Automation, and Economic Progress believes, will not alter the fact that by the turn of the century (within the lifetime of most of today's population) numerous changes will be required in work hours and leisure, in the structure of collective bargaining, in retirement and health provisions, and in other basic aspects of the industrial relations system. Even more drastic reforms may be required (although this is more speculative) by changes in the world community that may affect international labor standards, international labor organization and negotiations, and international labor requirements.

Finally, future developments in the United States and abroad may require research into the values on which labor and industrial relations are based. For example, what should be a firm's responsibilities toward its employees and to a community when it has decided to move its plant from one community to another? To what extent should the principles of industrial democracy be permitted to override the requirements of technology, bureaucracy, and efficiency? How far should the government go in protecting the interests of individual workers against the interests of companies and unions?

The role of research as an administrative tool in government, private industry, and unions may also be expected to increase. Social change creates numerous problems of adaptation for organizations, and the changes of a technological society tend to be more complex, more diversified, and more difficult to cope with. At the governmental level, laws such as those relating to workmen's compensation and health protection tend to become obsolete and need to be constantly revised to keep up with changes in the structure and operation of industry. An agency like the National Labor Relations Board often must change its conception of appropriate bargaining units because of the development of new products and the formation of new types of corporate and union organization. Because of changes in governmental policy toward the unemployed, the U.S. Employment Service must make changes in its administrative functions and procedures.

One of the policies of the Kennedy administration was the wide extension of cost-benefit studies to various governmental programs. Recognition of the importance of evaluating an agency's work in this way has been made far more explicit by the Johnson administration and will undoubtedly be intensified in the future. The chief limitation of the cost-benefit study is that many of the benefits (and some costs) of a governmental program cannot be translated into monetary terms. But quite apart from the comparison of benefits with costs, it is important to study the way a law or an administrative ruling or a court decision is translated into action. It is an old social science maxim that a written rule and its practical implementation are by no means synonymous. Moreover, as sociologists have discovered, administration often leads to unintended as well as intended consequences. Since relatively few evaluative studies have been made of governmental actions affecting labor, it is essential to sponsor more of them in the future. As examples of studies that might have fruitful results for improving administration, the following may be cited.

First, what are the effects of NLRB orders and penalties relating to unfair labor practices? Would different types of orders better effectuate the purposes of the act?

Second, how has the NLRB affected the process and content of collective bargaining? Should it be restricted to procedural issues?

Third, what would be the consequences of separating the employment service and unemployment insurance offices?

And fourth, how has the Landrum-Griffin Act affected the internal operations of local unions?

Whereas government, and particularly the federal government, has a long if erratic history of using research to improve administration in the labor field, neither the corporations nor the trade unions have made much progress in this regard. As some unions have demonstrated, research can increase understanding as to why certain categories of workers refuse to become union members and thereby can help improve organizing campaigns; it can reveal how members feel about union political activities or policies on race relations and thereby can influence leadership behavior; it can throw light on economic trends in the industries and markets with which a union is concerned and thereby can indicate the wage and fringe benefit levels which might be attained without adversely affecting the level of employment. In the same way, research can assist managements in assessing the success of a new incentive program or a change in personnel policies, in determining how to reduce labor turnover, or in identifying workers and first-line supervisors who have promotional possibilities. To what extent the corporations and the unions will utilize research for these and related purposes remains to be seen.

From the standpoint of developing a science, research in labor is still at the underdeveloped stage. It has not yet produced a solid theoretical foundation from which new questions and hypotheses can emerge. Its knowledge has grown in a purely haphazard and unrelated manner. The needed foundation may be provided if research is systematically pursued in each of the seven subdivisions of the labor field identified in Chapter V.

Labor history—Commons' famous study of the American shoemakers suggested a theory of industrial and labor development in the United States from colonial times to the end of the nineteenth century. This study ought to be replicated in other industries and its implications pursued into the twentieth century.

Union-management relations—Dunlop has offered a framework for the study of industrial relations systems. The framework raises more questions than it answers, but this is one of its values, and researchers should investigate empirically various of the assumptions and hypotheses that he makes regarding the interaction of specific environmental factors and particular working rules.

Public policy—although much has been learned about the formation of public policy, the effects of laws and orders have been largely neglected. A study of the impact of the NLRB, for example, on the scope of collective bargaining might throw light on the potential limits of union participation in management decision-making.

The labor market—since economic models of the labor market are well developed, the challenge in this area is to test various hypotheses about labor mobility, training, and wage payments, as well as to perform cost-benefit studies of programs based on them. An interesting question relating to the nature of work and employment is the feasibility of moving numbers of the so-called unemployables into the labor force.

Organizational behavior and interpersonal relations—this is another branch of the field in which theorizing seems to have overshadowed empirical research. Hence, there are innumerable hypotheses waiting to be tested in the works of March and Simon, Bakke and Argyris, Sayles and Strauss, Haire, Likert, Kahn, and others. The relationship between the needs of the individual and the objectives of the organization is worth a great deal of study. The process of organizational innovation or change remains, in the words of one expert, "the least developed aspect of organizational theory." Employee participation in decision-making has also become a topic of international concern.

Foreign labor and international comparisons—in this area, descriptive and interpretative research, mostly of an impressionistic nature, has proceeded with little theoretical orientation. Perhaps this is inevitable since a sound factual foundation is ordinarily essential to sound theory. A problem that needs close study is the extent to which international labor standards, such as those adopted by the International Labor Organization, can be successfully implemented in newly industrializing nations. The answer might help distinguish between the universal and the culture-bound elements of the field.

Industrial society—this is the area of the classical tradition—the grand theorists and social philosophers —but C. Wright Mills and Reinhard Bendix have shown how large social questions can be explored and general propositions developed by a combination of microanalysis and macroanalysis. One of the major research problems is whether, in a technological society, democratic processes can survive. At the micro level, there are intriguing questions about the appropriate balance between work and leisure, the possibilities of redesigning work and machines so as to maximize the creativity and self-expression of workers, and the psychology of money as a work incentive.[2]

Concepts and Theories

As the preceding discussion has indicated at several points, it is this author's strong conviction that one of the major tasks of researchers in the future is the development of a more adequate body of concepts and theories. Conceptualization is likely to receive proper consideration only if the underlying logic of a research project is subjected to rigorous scrutiny, or if the operational requirements of a project call for systematic data collection and precise measurement.

As long as research is conducted on an impressionistic and qualitative basis, there is a tendency for the key concepts to be treated rather loosely. But quantification is by no means the panacea, although standardized measurements wherever possible are of great value to the researcher. When certain concepts do not lend themselves readily to quantitative treatment, they may be reduced to less sophisticated terms in order to facilitate quantification. This pragmatic compromise is found in many labor studies, often to the detriment of the conclusions. Thus, the key to conceptualization is a conscious awareness of its importance. The creation of new concepts or the "original" redefinition of old ones to deal with dynamic conditions is the lifeblood of a scientific field, but this process appears to be essentially an act of imagination for which no existing rules can substitute.

Concepts and theories are closely interrelated. Theory consists of statements about concepts that describe their interrelationship and asserts or predicts how a change in one will affect another. It seems reasonable to expect labor researchers to make increasing use of theory as a guide to their research. The overly simple empiricism of past decades in American social science is declining, to judge from the research reports in the various professional journals. Since industrial relations theory is strongly influenced by theorizing in the several social science disciplines, the development of theory in these disciplines is bound to be contagious. Another healthy influence in this respect is the growing interchange between labor scholars in the United States and those in foreign countries, particularly Europe. Although this interchange is negligible in comparison with developments in the physical sciences, it is having the effect of blending American traditions of pragmatism and European traditions of theorizing to the mutual benefit of both.

Impact of the Computer

Future labor research, like all of the social sciences, can expect to be influenced by the revolution in electronic computers. The first and most obvious effect is on data processing and analysis. The ability to handle masses of data and large numbers of variables will make it possible, for example, to use the vast collection of governmental statistics that have been only partially analyzed in the past. Historians, legal scholars, political scientists, and other specialists in documentary study should also benefit from the information retrieval capabilities of the computers. The computers should facilitate the content analysis of masses of qualitative materials and permit summary statements to be expressed in numbers.

New tools, however, invariably have more fundamental effects on scientific study; they make it possible to select problems and design them in ways which would not have been feasible previously. Thus, systems analysis and multivariate regression models as well as comprehensive international comparisons would appear to be in the offing on a significant scale. The physical scientists and the econometricians have already demonstrated the potentialities.

The computers also make it possible, as Simon and his colleagues at Carnegie Tech have shown, to simulate various aspects of the real world and to conduct laboratory experiments of organizational and interpersonal behavior. Some stimulating work has already been done in the areas of bargaining and decision-making. More should follow.

Finally, the computers should lead to more rigorous problem formulation since it is possible to use them as a logic machine and to explore the implications of various assumptions, postulates, and hypotheses.

Training for Research

The pre-World War II students of labor problems for the most part were not methodologically oriented as far as research was concerned. They approached research largely from a common sense, pragmatic standpoint. Since 1945, the field has become more method conscious, and it is reasonable to anticipate that this awareness will continue to grow and be reflected in the training that new students will receive, especially at the graduate level. As William F. Whyte stated in a 1960 address:

You might say that we have tended to be methodologically muscle-bound. The general rule has been: one man, one method. At least in the past you tended to learn the questionnaire-survey approach or a more anthropological type of approach and whatever it was you learned, you followed. You let the method dictate how you sized up a problem and went at it rather than letting the problem dictate the method.[3]

An examination of the M.A. and Ph.D. curricula in industrial relations reveals a growing effort to develop the student's methodological abilities on a broader basis. As previously noted, at the University of Illinois, for example, the Ph.D. candidate is required to take a semester course in the logic or theory of social science research and a year-long course in quantitative research methods beyond introductory statistics, as well as to gain an intimate knowledge of the methodology of two specific disciplines.

This interdisciplinary approach to a broader training in research methods is developing at a time when the separate disciplines are intensifying their methodological efforts. The psychologists and sociologists have for some time been the leaders in this movement. The economists, who are among the most sophisticated in the area of statistics, are placing much more stress on field methods. And the political scientists and lawyers, traditionally the least sensitive to research methodology, except in the analysis of documents at which they are expert, have begun to think seriously about research training.

There are, of course, limits to what can be accomplished by teaching *about* research. No discussion or textbook can serve the function that direct involvement in research under the guidance of an experienced researcher can provide. Hence, research training must interrelate the classroom with the field or laboratory project. The establishment of social science survey centers, pioneered by the Universities of Michigan, Columbia, and Chicago, will be a valuable adjunct to the training of labor researchers as well as other social scientists. The computer centers and the operations research and general systems analysis units found at an ever-increasing number of universities offer an equal opportunity.

Relations Between the Academicians and the Operators

The relations between academic researchers and the participants in labor affairs—union leaders, corporate managers, and government officials—are much more crucial to the success of research than are comparable relations in most other fields, social as well as physical. One reason is obvious: the participants control most of the raw data, and unless they are willing to cooperate, research possibilities are sharply curtailed. But there are additional, more subtle reasons. Among the participants are numerous highly knowledgeable and insightful individuals who have much to contribute to the research process and who should be involved in it wherever feasible. Moreover, the decision to undertake research is not purely an academic decision even when academicians are doing the research. The recent growth of government-sponsored labor research and more limited programs sponsored by corporations and unions are only a forerunner of a more extensive development in the future. Furthermore, the government and the private parties will make increasing use of academicians as consultants in labor research by their own staffs.

Hence, the relations between the academic and outside worlds need much more consideration than they have had. One set of interesting questions involves the types of research that are best done on campus as contrasted to those best done by the government or private organizations. The primary responsibility for the development of an industrial relations science undoubtedly must lie with the academics, whereas administration-oriented research is the responsibility of the organizations. The organizations must be alert to the need for change and ought, therefore, to be constantly conducting cost-benefit and other evaluative studies to improve themselves. However, self-appraisal may not always raise the most critical questions, and more objective research, particularly as it applies to matters of public concern, may flow from the inquiries of the university faculties. In theory, the universities are best equipped to identify and formulate important research problems, to develop concepts and hypotheses, to explore and challenge the prevailing values of society and the participants in labor matters —although it must be added that they have not lived up to their potential in these respects. The governmental agencies are best equipped in terms of finances and manpower to be the basic fact finders, although there are some types of facts (especially of a subjective or informal nature) where the academician has the advantage. The corporations and unions are in the best position to˙ conduct experiments with different policies and to test out relevant hypotheses; they, too, have access to certain types of organization data that are ordinarily not available to others.

This division of responsibility is not intended to be exclusive; there is room and need for extensive crossover of function. As experience has shown, an intermixture of personnel often provides the best results. In order to be sensitive to the problems of public and institutional life, academicians should be in constant touch with government agencies, unions, and employers—as consultants, as temporary employees, as contractual or invited researchers. Similarly, the operating agencies in government and industry should be sending their most imaginative personnel to the academic community to learn the latest developments in the social sciences, to take time off from their operating functions so that they can think, write, and teach in a different kind of environment with a different set of time and job perspectives.

In a recent paper presented to the University Labor Education Association, Don Vial, chairman of the Center for Labor Research and Education, Institute of Industrial Relations, University of California at Berkeley, made a powerful case for integrating union service research with labor education services of uni-

versities. Vial noted the wide gap presently existing
between the "academic" research of faculty members
and the "adversary" research of union staff officials.
In order to make university research useful to the
unions, he argued, faculty members who are interested
in applied, action-oriented research ought to teach in
the programs of the labor centers and not stay aloof
as many do now. This integration would give more
realism to the selection and formulation of problems,
would build union confidence in the researchers, and
would make available union data not heretofore
provided. For the unions, it would afford a clearer
identification of educational needs and program development and would enable the unions to approach
industry and community problems with greater understanding and effectiveness.[4]

To an increasing degree, government, industry, and
labor are employing well-trained research people who
can communicate with the academicians in a common
technical language and with a common understanding
of the values and limitations of research. One of the
important tasks of the future is to train organizational
executives to acquire a more sophisticated understanding of what researchers can and cannot be expected
to accomplish. This subject has been analyzed in a
brilliant essay by Max Millikan explaining the frequent disappointments of executives who have not
received expected answers to their problems from
research and the frustrations of researchers who have
not obtained the proper involvement of the executives.
He observes:

Social science research on a problem can illuminate the
variety of forces at work, can place limits on the range of
possible outcomes, can force implicit, partial judgments
into explicit form in which they can be systematically ex-

amined and their applicability tested, and can explore the
internal consistency of a variety of intuitive expectations.
Most policy judgments involve an implicit appraisal of
resources, of motivations, of organizational and administrative possibilities, of political interests, and the like. Economic, psychological, political, and sociological analysis can
expose these judgments to systematic scrutiny. Their combination into an estimate of the situation as a whole will
almost always require a process that goes beyond the limits
of "scientific" analysis, but such analysis can enormously
strengthen the validity of the intuitive process.[5]

A final brief word on values is appropriate. Most
labor research, except for some of the reformist variety,
has been based on the assumption that the prevailing
values of the society and of its chief institutional com-
ponents—government, corporations, unions—are in-
trinsically sound and that the problems to be resolved
are primarily of a technical nature. This will no
doubt continue to be true in the future. It is vital,
however, to any scientific field that its underlying
assumptions should always be subject to critical appraisal and, if necessary, to challenge. Postwar labor
research has reflected very little of such challenge. It
is to be hoped that among future researchers there
will be at least a few who will regard this as their
major function.

APPENDIX

Outline

of an Introductory

Research Course

Since 1948, this author has given a semester course to first-year graduate students that is intended to introduce them to the nature of research in the labor field.[1] The purpose of the course is twofold: to provide a sufficient understanding of the research process so that the students can read the research literature with a critical and perceptive eye, and to indicate the aspects of research that the researcher must take into account if he is to perform his task effectively. The outline of this course may help illuminate the discussion on methodology in this volume. Since the assigned readings (which have changed frequently over the years) will not be given, except by occasional example, it should be observed that the basic approach is applicable to social science research in general, but that the substantive aspects deal with labor and industrial relations problems, and both concepts and methods are interdisciplinary in character. A semester course in statistics is a prerequisite; a year course would be preferable.

In the following discussion, different areas are covered and a brief description of each is given.

Modes of problem-solving—The initial discussion is designed to make clear that problems may be resolved in a variety of ways—reliance on experience or custom, common sense, trial-and-error, etc.—of which research is only one. Because of its cost in time, money, and manpower, research should be used only when the other approaches promise to be unsuccessful, and the nature of the problem lends itself to empirical exploration.

Alternative research processes—Once the decision to undertake research is made, recognition must be given to the fact that there is no one research methodology but a number of methodologies, depending on the nature of the problem and the stage of knowledge surrounding it. The perceptive discussion of F.S.C. Northrop in his influential book, *The Logic of the Sciences and the Humanities,* is useful here. But it is also important to note that approaches will differ for other reasons, such as the researcher's temperament and training, his possible attachment to a particular set of techniques, and his inclination to follow what C. Wright Mills called the classical tradition or the more limited approach of the pragmatist. The general stages of research—problem formulation, data collection, data analysis and interpretation, and report writing and transmittal—are outlined, with special stress on the interweaving and circular nature of research in practice as opposed to the straight line, step-by-step cookbook procedure.

An overall framework—The final introductory phase is intended to make the student realize that every researcher, consciously or not, operates within a personal system of value-premises about: the nature of man, the nature of society, the nature of knowledge, and the nature of the process of acquiring knowledge. It is essential for the student to understand and make explicit his own values on these philosophical issues as well as to appreciate the wide range of different values that researchers may hold.

Problem formulation—As Northrop and others have stressed, the most important aspect of research is its beginning because it so strongly influences all subsequent action. This assumption is adopted even though it is recognized that the whole course of research and the most significant findings may sometimes be affected later by chance or unexpected discoveries and occurrences. The meaning of a problem is explored, and the reduction of the problematic situation, to use John Dewey's terms, to the relevant factual situation is analyzed. This process entails such elements as problem definition and delimitation, the identification and operational definition of key concepts, the explicit statement of the assumptions on which inquiry rests, and the determination as to the direction that the search for facts should take—that is, the hypotheses to be tested or the key questions to be pursued. The sophisticated discussion on concepts by Abraham Kaplan in *The Conduct of Inquiry* is worth close study.

Assumptions and values—Because they are so often overlooked by both researchers and readers, assumptions and values are given special discussion in a separate class session. The issue of value-free social science—as raised many decades ago by Max Weber and as debated by contemporary social scientists like George A. Lundberg, Gunnar Myrdal, and Alvin Gouldner—and questions of objectivity and existentialism are examined.

Theories, hypotheses, and questions—Another aspect of problem formulation that needs special attention because the typical academic treatment of it diverges so often from research practice in the labor field deals with the role of theory. The ideal model of research, derived from stereotypes of the physical sciences, posits the statement of a theory of either an axiomatic or empirical nature from which hypotheses are deduced and subjected to empirical verification or refutation. In practice, only a small minority of labor research projects are conducted on this basis. For the most part, researchers have either found no worthwhile theory available to guide them or have preferred to proceed on the basis of hunches, impressionistic judgments, or the findings of other researchers. It is therefore important to consider the conditions under which research should be theory directed, the problems involved in using grand theories of the classical tradition or more modest theories of what Robert K. Merton has called the middle range, the advantages and disadvantages of hypotheses that are not derived from a more general theory, and the method of key questions in lieu of theory or hypothesis.

Study design—This phase of research is concerned with how the facts or evidence essential to the resolution of the problem are to be gathered. Although no satisfactory system of classifying study designs has been developed, the existence of a wide variety of designs is recognized, and decisions must be made by every researcher as to which design is most suitable to his problem. Despite the practical consideration that many researchers are essentially one-design or one-method specialists, and the favored design or method in effect shapes the problem, the more logical principle is that methodology should be tailored to a problem. Because of time limitations, the course concentrates on the following study designs: the case study, the comparative study, the sample survey, and the controlled experiment. In each instance, differing versions of the basic design are assessed, and criteria for selection—such as relevancy to the problem, available monetary and technical resources, and feasibility —are considered.

Data collection techniques—It is difficult to isolate the data collection techniques from the study design, but the more detailed aspects of the techniques should be treated separately. Techniques—documentary content analysis, personal observation, interviewing, questionnaire construction, sampling design and administration—are not easily taught in the classroom, apart from an actual project, or in a short time. Nonetheless, some exposure to the literature and some discussion of basic principles and operating problems may be enlightening to the student.

Facts and errors—Particularly important in respect to data collection is a discussion of the nature of facts, of the ingredients that go into the construction of a statement of fact; that is, concepts, symbols, perceptions, premises, and inferences or interpretative judgments based on a preponderance of evidence. Likewise, attention is devoted to the nature of error, the sources or causes of error in research, and methods for reducing error. Oscar Morgenstern's *On the Accuracy of Economic Observations* is a valuable reference.

Data analysis and interpretation—The mass of raw evidence that is gathered must, of course, be summarized and related in a meaningful way to the questions or hypotheses generated in the problem formulation stage. Both quantitative and qualitative methods of analysis are treated, including problems of classification, coding, and electronic machine utilization. The matter of causal analysis, of extracting meanings from the data beyond description and correlation, is given considerable emphasis. The dangers of generalization beyond the level warranted by the data, so often ignored by labor researchers, are noted.

Research and policy-making—The final session[2] is devoted to the intricate relationships between researchers and policy-makers in various types of organizations outside of the academic world. The often erroneous expectations of both sides, as discussed so perceptively by Max Millikan, are assessed, and the nature of realistic expectations is considered. Certain ethical problems which may arise in a controversial field like labor are analyzed.

In giving such a course to students of labor problems, it is important to interweave the basic writings of social scientists and philosophers who are not particularly concerned with the labor field,[3] the general writings on research methodology of labor researchers, and examples (in article or book form) of labor research projects. It has also been found extremely profitable to have each student undertake the design of a research project on the basis of a problem with which he has already familiarized himself in other courses or in work experience.

Notes

CHAPTER I

The Domain of Labor Problems Research

1. Neil W. Chamberlain, "Issues for the Future," *Proceedings of the Thirteenth Annual Meeting of the Industrial Relations Research Association,* December 28–29, 1960, p. 101.

2. Arthur M. Ross, "Labor Courses: The Need for Radical Reconstruction," *Industrial Relations,* 4 (October, 1964), 7.

3. Milton Derber and Rennard Davis, "Research at the Industrial Relations Centers," *Proceedings of the Fifteenth Annual Meeting of the Industrial Relations Research Association,* December 27–28, 1962, pp. 107–198.

4. See Clarence J. Hicks, *My Life in Industrial Relations* (New York: Harper, 1941), pp. 117–119, and Chap. VIII.

5. In a 1964 survey by Max S. Wortman, Jr., only 43 of the nation's 80 largest manufacturing corporations reported that they engaged in industrial relations research, mostly of an "applied" character. Twenty firms reported no such research, and 17 refused to respond. "Corporate Industrial Relations Research—Dream or Reality," *Academy of Management Journal,* Vol. 9, No. 2, 1966.

6. *Proceedings of Fifth Annual Meeting of Industrial Relations Research Association,* December 28–29, 1952, p. 6.

7. Sumner H. Slichter, James J. Healy, and E. Robert Livernash, *The Impact of Collective Bargaining on Management* (Washington, D.C.: Brookings, 1960), p. 6.

8. John T. Dunlop, *Industrial Relations Systems* (New York: Henry Holt, 1958), p. vi.

9. Robert S. Lynd, *Knowledge For What* (Princeton: Princeton University Press, 1948).

10. Milton Derber, "Divergent Tendencies in Industrial Relations Research," *Industrial and Labor Relations Review,* 17 (July, 1964), 609–611.
11. Bureau of National Affairs, *Daily Labor Reports,* October 21, 1965, No. 204, E-1.

CHAPTER II

Origins in Reformism

1. Jonathan Grossman, *William Sylvis, Pioneer of American Labor* (New York: Columbia University Press, 1945), pp. 255–256.
2. Wright's career and influence are admirably described in James Leiby, *Carroll Wright and Labor Reform* (Cambridge: Harvard University Press, 1960).
3. *Ibid.,* p. 95.
4. Richard T. Ely, *The Labor Movement in America* (New York: Crowell, 1886), p. v.
5. *Ibid.*
6. Richard T. Ely, *An Introduction to Political Economy* (New York: Hunt and Eaton, 1889), pp. 236–239.
7. John R. Commons, reprinted in his *Labor and Administration* (New York: Macmillan, 1913), pp. 7–13.
8. John R. Commons, Reprinted in *Labor and Administration,* pp. 1–6.
9. U.S. Commission on Industrial Relations, *Final Report* (Washington, D.C.: Barnard & Miller, printers, 1915), p. 308.
10. Cover page of first issue, *Charities and the Commons,* Vol. XXII, No. 1 (April 3, 1909).
11. *Ibid.,* pp. v and vi.
12. Henry W. Farnam, *The Survey,* XXIII (January 15, 1910), 528.
13. Harry W. Laidler, ed., *Forty Years of Education,* a symposium published by the League for Industrial Democracy, New York, June, 1945.
14. Reprinted in *The Survey,* XXVII (December 30, 1911), 1431.
15. *Final Report of the Commission on Industrial Relations,* p. 1.
16. "The Idea of Industrial Democracy in America, 1898–1915," *Labor History,* Vol. 7, No. 3 (Fall, 1966); "The Idea of Industrial Democracy in America, 1915–1935," *Labor History,* Vol. 8, No. 1 (Winter, 1967); and " 'Industrial Democracy' As an Organizing Concept for a Theory of Industrial Relations"

(mimeo), Institute of Labor and Industrial Relations, University of Illinois, 1966.

17. In 1957, the Fund established a Center for the Study of Democratic Institutions in Santa Barbara, California. The corporation and the trade union were selected as two of six major institutions to be studied. A series of conferences, papers, and monographs was promoted by the center.

CHAPTER III

Research as an Instrument of Administration

1. See Lafayette G. Harter, Jr., *John R. Commons: His Assault on Laissez-faire* (Corvallis, Oregon: Oregon State University Press, 1962).

2. *Ibid.*, pp. 341 and 342.

3. *Report of the Eight-Hour Commission* (Washington: Government Printing Office, 1918), p. 4.

4. The material in this and the following paragraph is taken from Gordon S. Watkins, *Labor Problems and Labor Administration in the United States During the World War* (Urbana: University of Illinois, 1919).

5. *Ibid.*, p. 217.

6. The American Society of Mechanical Engineers, *Fifty Years Progress in Management, 1910–1960* (New York: ASME, 1960), p. 294.

7. *Ibid.*, p. 279.

8. A lively and provocative account of the development of industrial psychology in the United States is to be found in Loren Baritz, *The Servants of Power* (Middletown, Connecticut: Wesleyan University Press, 1960). A much more condensed and more sympathetic discussion is by Leonard W. Ferguson, "The Development of Industrial Psychology," in B. von Haller Gilmer, *Industrial Psychology* (New York: McGraw-Hill, 1961), Chap. 2.

9. J. B. S. Hardman and Maurice F. Neufeld, *The House of Labor* (New York: Prentice-Hall, 1951), p. 230.

10. Bureau of Labor Statistics, U. S. Department of Labor, *Directory of National and International Labor Unions in the United States*, 1965, Bulletin No. 1493, p. 63.

11. Hardman and Neufeld, *op. cit.*, pp. 242–249.

12. Industrial Relations Research Association, *Proceedings of the Tenth Annual Meeting*, September 5–7, 1957, p. 254.

13. *Ibid.*, pp. 249–253.
14. Referred to in Jack Barbash, *The Practice of Unionism* (New York: Harper, 1956), p. 280.
15. Hjalmar Rosen and R. A. Hudson Rosen, *The Union Member Speaks* (New York: Prentice-Hall, 1955).

CHAPTER IV

Toward the Development of a Science

1. Jacob H. Hollander and George E. Barnett, eds., *Studies in American Trade Unionism* (New York: Henry Holt, 1912), p. 5.
2. *Report of the Industrial Commission* (Washington: Government Printing Office, 1901), Vol. VII, 16.
3. Carroll Wright, "Contributions of the United States Government to Social Science," *American Journal of Sociology*, 1 (November, 1895), 242.
4. Carroll D. Wright, "The Evolution of Wage Statistics," *Quarterly Journal of Economics*, VI (January, 1892), 151–189.
5. Wesley C. Mitchell, *The Making and Using of Index Numbers*, Part I in U.S. Department of Labor, Bureau of Labor Statistics, Bulletin No. 173 (Washington: Government Printing Office, 1915), pp. 7–8.
6. Paul Douglas, *Real Wages in the United States, 1890–1926* (Boston: Houghton, 1930), and *The Theory of Wages* (New York: Macmillan, 1934).
7. John I. Griffin, *Strikes: A Study in Quantitative Economics* (New York: Columbia University Press, 1939).
8. Leo Wolman, *Ebb and Flow in Trade Unionism* (New York: National Bureau of Economic Research, 1936) and *The Growth of American Trade Unions, 1880–1923* (New York: National Bureau of Economic Research, 1924).
9. John R. Commons, reprinted in *Labor and Administration* (New York: Macmillan, 1913).
10. Lloyd Ulman, *The Rise of the National Trade Union* (Cambridge: Harvard University Press, 1955).
11. Selig Perlman, *A Theory of the Labor Movement* (New York: Macmillan, 1928).
12. John R. Commons, *Industrial Government* (New York: Macmillan, 1921).
13. John R. Commons, *Myself* (New York: Macmillan, 1934), p. 93.

14. Robert F. Hoxie, *Trade Unionism in the United States,* 2nd ed. (New York: Appleton, 1931), pp. 58–59.

15. Commons, *op. cit.,* p. 179.

16. Carleton Parker, *The Casual Laborer and Other Essays* (New York: Harcourt, Brace and Howe, 1920), p. 59.

17. Frederick W. Taylor, *The Principles of Scientific Management* (New York: Harper, 1911), pp. 54–55.

18. The detailed description of the Hawthorne experiments is found in F. J. Roethlisberger and William J. Dickson, *Management and the Worker* (Cambridge: Harvard University Press, 1949).

19. Described in James G. Mills, ed., *Experiments in Social Process* (New York: McGraw-Hill, 1950), Chap. 6. The president of Harwood, Alfred J. Marrow, was a Ph.D. student of Lewin's.

20. Clarence D. Long, *The Labor Force Under Changing Income and Employment* (Princeton: Princeton University Press, 1958); Jacob Mincer, "Labor Force Participation of Married Women," *Aspects of Labor Economics,* National Bureau of Economic Research (Princeton: Princeton University Press, 1962); Lee Hansen, "The Cycloid Sensitivity of the Labor Supply," *American Economic Review* (June, 1961).

21. Gary Becker, *Human Capital* (New York: National Bureau of Economic Research, 1965).

22. Paul H. Douglas, *The Theory of Wages* (New York: Macmillan, 1934); Walter A. Fogel, "Job Rate Ranges: A Theoretical and Empirical Analysis," *Industrial and Labor Relations Review,* Vol. 17, No. 4 (July, 1964).

CHAPTER V

Expanding Knowledge and Current Gaps

1. More detailed descriptions of recent research may be found in such publications of the Industrial Relations Research Association as *A Decade of Industrial Relations Research, 1946–1956* (New York: Harper, 1958), *Research in Industrial Human Relations* (New York: Harper, 1957), and *Employment Relation Research* (New York: Harper, 1960).

2. Except where some discussion follows, no attempt will be made to provide citations of the works mentioned in this chapter. On labor history, the reader is referred to two excellent bibliographical sources: Gene S. Stroud and Gilbert E. Donahue, *Labor History in the United States* (Urbana:

Institute of Labor and Industrial Relations, University of Illinois, 1961), Bibliographic Contributions No. 6; and Maurice F. Neufeld, *A Representative Bibliography of American Labor History* (Ithaca: New York State School of Industrial and Labor Relations, Cornell University, 1964).

3. Mark Perlman, *Labor Union Theories in America* (Evanston: Row, Peterson, 1958).

4. James D. Morris, *Conflict Within the AFL: A Study of Craft Versus Industrial Unionism, 1901–1938* (Ithaca: Cornell, 1958).

5. For more detailed expressions of this view, see the discussion "Labor History," in Industrial Relations Research Association, *Proceedings of the Eighteenth Annual Meeting*, December 28–29, 1965 (New York: IRRA, 1966), pp. 324–354.

6. Harry A. Millis, *How Collective Bargaining Works* (New York: Twentieth Century Fund, 1942).

7. John T. Dunlop and William F. Whyte, "Framework for the Analysis of Industrial Relations: Two Views," *Industrial and Labor Relations Review*, 3 (April, 1950), 383–412.

8. The literature on power outside of the labor relations field is, of course, tremendous. The political scientists and sociologists, in particular, have written extensively on the subject. More recently the psychologists have turned their attention to the subject, as witness, Dorwin Cartwright, ed., *Studies in Social Power*, 2nd ed. (Ann Arbor: University of Michigan, 1959); Robert L. Kahn and Elise Boulding, eds., *Power and Conflict in Organizations* (New York: Basic Books, 1964).

9. James W. Kuhn, *Bargaining in Grievance Settlement* (New York: Columbia University Press, 1961), p. 167.

10. See for example, Industrial Relations Research Association, *Power in Industrial Relations: Its Use and Abuse*, Proceedings of Spring Meeting, St. Louis, Missouri, May 2–3, 1958.

11. Neil Chamberlain, *The Union Challenge to Management Control* (New York: Harper, 1948).

12. John Dunlop, *Industrial Relations Systems* (New York: Holt-Dryden, 1958).

13. Richard E. Walton and Robert B. McKersie, *A Behavioral Theory of Labor Negotiations* (New York: McGraw-Hill, 1965). The interdisciplinary character of this book and its wide-ranging references are worth noting.

14. Richard C. Cortner, *The Wagner Act Cases* (Knoxville: University of Tennessee Press, 1964).

15. Herbert S. Parnes, *Research on Labor Mobility: An Appraisal of Research Findings in the United States,* Bulletin 65 (New York: Social Science Research Council, 1954).

16. Lloyd G. Reynolds and Cynthia H. Taft, *The Evolution of Wage Structure* (New Haven: Yale University Press, 1956).

17. H. Gregg Lewis, *Unionism and Relative Wages in the United States* (Chicago: University of Chicago Press, 1963).

18. A. W. Phillips, "The Relation Between Unemployment and the Rate of Change of Money Wage Rates in the United Kingdom, 1862–1957," *Economica,* Vol. XXV (November, 1958). The so-called Phillips curve was a pioneering effort to demonstrate statistically a rather close relationship between the percentage change in money wage rates and the unemployment rate in a national economy. An elaboration of Phillips' study was R. G. Lipsey, "The Relation Between Unemployment and the Rate of Change of Money Wage Rates in the United Kingdom, 1862–1957: A Further Analysis," *Economica,* Vol. XXVII (February, 1960).

19. See *Studies in Unemployment* and a huge supplemental volume, *Readings in Unemployment,* printed for the Special Committee pursuant to S. Res. 196, 86th Congress, 2nd Session (Washington: Government Printing Office, 1960).

20. National Commission on Technology, Automation, and Economic Progress, *Technology and the American Economy,* Vol. 1 (February, 1966).

21. For the most recent statement, see the Introduction to the second edition of his *Bonds of Organization* (Hamden, Connecticut: Archon Books, 1966). The latest of the many Argyris volumes is *Organization and Innovation* (Homewood, Illinois: Irwin-Dorsey, 1965).

22. Douglas McGregor, *The Human Side of Enterprise* (New York: McGraw-Hill, 1960).

23. Peter Drucker, *The New Society* (New York: Harper, 1950, 1962).

24. Melville Dalton, *Men Who Manage: Fusions of Feeling and Theory in Administration* (New York: Wiley, 1959).

25. See Rensis Likert, *New Patterns of Management* (New York: McGraw-Hill, 1961) and Robert L. Kahn *et al., Organizational Stress: Studies in Role Conflict and Ambiguity* (New York: Wiley, 1964).

26. Victor H. Vroom, *Work and Motivation* (New York: Wiley, 1964).

27. For a brief summary of some of the more recent research in this area, see Harry C. Triandis, "Notes on the Design of Organizations," James D. Thompson, ed., *Approaches to Organizational Design* (Pittsburgh: University of Pittsburgh Press, 1966), Chap. 2.

28. For a recent reference, see James D. Thompson, ed., *Approaches to Organizational Design* (Pittsburgh: University of Pittsburgh Press, 1966).

29. See, for example, their books *The Local Union: Its Place in the Industrial Plant* (New York: Harper, 1953) and *Human Behavior in Organizations* (Englewood Cliffs, New Jersey: Prentice-Hall, 1966).

30. *Leadership Dynamics and the Trade-Union Leader* (New York: New York University Press, 1959).

31. Seymour M. Lipset, Martin A. Trow, and James S. Coleman, *Union Democracy: The Internal Politics of the International Typographical Union* (Glencoe, Illinois: The Free Press, 1956).

32. Arnold S. Tannenbaum and Robert L. Kahn, *Participation in Local Unions* (Evanston: Row, Peterson, 1958), p. 237.

33. The crowning volume of this project was Clark Kerr *et al.*, *Industrialism and Industrial Man* (Cambridge: Harvard University Press, 1960).

34. Both the Garbarino report and a brief summation of the Edelman-Fleming study are contained in Arthur M. Ross, ed., *Employment Policy and the Labor Market* (Berkeley: University of California Press, 1965).

35. *Ibid.*, p. 4. A notable illustration of this stimulating force is the 1966 conference sponsored by the Center for the Study of Democratic Institutions to discuss the penetrating critique by the French social philosopher Jacques Ellul, *The Technological Society* (New York: Knopf, 1965).

CHAPTER VI

Methodological Problems

1. Industrial Relations Research Association, *Proceedings of the Eighteenth Annual Winter Meeting*, New York, December 28–29, 1965, p. 162.

2. See Neil Chamberlain, *Labor* (New York: McGraw-Hill, 1958), Chap. 12.

3. Margaret Chandler, *Management Rights and Union Interests* (New York: McGraw-Hill, 1964), pp. 3–6.

4. Industrial Relations Research Association, *Proceedings of the Eighteenth Annual Winter Meeting*, New York, December 28–29, 1965, p. 193.

5. *The Industrial Psychologist, Division 14, Newsletter*, American Psychological Association, 3 (November, 1965), 33.

6. E. Wight Bakke and Chris Argyris, *Organizational Structure and Dynamics: A Framework for Theory* (New Haven: Yale, 1954), p. 1.

7. James D. Thompson, ed., *Approaches to Organizational Design* (Pittsburgh: University of Pittsburgh Press, 1966), p. 219.

8. *Ibid.*, p. 3.

9. Lloyd Reynolds, *The Structure of Labor Markets* (New York: Harper, 1951), pp. 230 and 245.

10. I am indebted to Professor Stuart Altman for this example.

11. For an interesting account of the Harwood research, see Alfred J. Marrow, "Risks and Uncertainties in Action Research," *The Journal of Social Issues*, XX (July, 1964), 15–20.

12. Melville Dalton, "Communication: Union-Management Relations Research," *Industrial and Labor Relations Review*, 14 (April, 1961), 456.

13. See Robert M. Macdonald, "An Evaluation of the Economic Analysis of Unionism," *Industrial and Labor Relations Review*, 19 (April, 1966), 347.

14. See Murray Edelman, "The Conceptual Frameworks of Normatively Oriented Empirically Based Research," May, 1966 (mimeo).

15. *Proceedings of First Annual Meeting*, December, 1948, p. 15.

16. *Proceedings of Fifth Annual Meeting*, December, 1952, p. 6.

17. *Proceedings of Fifteenth Annual Meeting*, December, 1962, p. 8.

18. *Proceedings of Seventeenth Annual Meeting*, December, 1964, p. 7.

19. George W. Hartmann and Theodore Newcomb, eds., *Industrial Conflict: A Psychological Interpretation* (New York: Cordon, 1939), pp. vi and vii.

20. Loren Baritz, *The Servants of Power* (Middletown, Conneticut: Wesleyan University Press, 1960).

21. An interesting example of replication is the Norwegian study on employee participation in instituting production changes which repeated the Coch and French experiments at Har-

wood. See John R. P. French, Jr., Joachim Israel, and Dagfinn
As, "An Experiment on Participation in a Norwegian Fac-
tory: Interpersonal Dimensions of Decision-Making," *Human
Relations*, Vol. 13, No. 1 (February, 1960).

CHAPTER VII

Prospects for the Future

1. A new periodical, *The Journal of Human Resources*, devoted
   to education, manpower, and welfare policies, appeared in
   1966 under the sponsorship of the Industrial Relations Research Institute and the Center for Studies in Vocational and
   Technical Education, University of Wisconsin.
2. On this latter topic, see Mason Haire, Edwin E. Ghiselli, and
   Lyman W. Porter, "Psychological Research on Pay: An Over-
   view," *Industrial Relations*, 3 (October, 1963) 3–8.
3. William F. Whyte, "Needs and Opportunities for Industrial
   Relations Research," New York State School of Industrial and
   Labor Relations at Cornell University, Reprint Series No.
   125, p. 6.
4. Don Vial, "Comments on the Research Functions of University
   Labor Centers," ULEA Annual Conference, Detroit, Michigan,
   March 30–April 1, 1966 (mimeo., 28 pp.).
5. Max Millikan, "Inquiry and Policy: The Relations of Knowledge to Action," in Daniel Lerner, ed., *The Human Meaning
   of the Social Sciences* (Cleveland: World Publishing, Meridian
   Books, 1959), p. 166.

Appendix

1. Since 1958, my colleague, Professor Walter Franke, has shared the responsibility with me and helped shape the content of this course.
2. Time permitting, the course should devote some attention to the preparation of a research report properly designed for a given audience. Unfortunately, a semester is usually too short for adequate treatment of this subject and reliance has to be placed on guidance in other courses.
3. Among the numerous writings on social science methodology, the following are good representative examples:

Russell L. Ackoff, *The Design of Social Research* (Chicago: University of Chicago Press, 1953).

E. H. Carr, *What is History?* (London: Penguin Books, 1964).

Leon Festinger and Daniel Katz, *Research Methods in the Behavioral Sciences* (New York: Dryden, 1953).

Robert L. Kahn and Charles F. Cannell, *The Dynamics of Interviewing* (New York: Wiley, 1957).

Abraham Kaplan, *The Conduct of Inquiry* (San Francisco: Chandler, 1964).

Daniel Lerner, ed., *The Human Meaning of the Social Sciences* (Cleveland: Meridian Books, 1959).

R. M. MacIver, *Social Causation* (New York: Harper Torchbooks, 1964).

C. Wright Mills, *The Sociological Imagination* (New York: Grove, 1961).

Oscar Morgenstern, *On the Accuracy of Economic Observations,* second edition (Princeton: Princeton University Press, 1963).

F. S. C. Northrop, *The Logic of the Sciences and the Humanities* (New York: Macmillan, 1948).

Karl R. Popper, *The Poverty of Historicism* (New York: Hayer Torchbooks, 1964).

Bernard S. Phillips, *Social Research* (New York: Macmillan, 1966).

Claire Selltiz *et al., Research Methods in Social Relations* (New York: Henry Holt, 1959).

Pauline V. Young, *Scientific Social Surveys and Research* (Englewood Cliffs, New Jersey: Prentice-Hall, 1956).

Index

Academic research, 8–9, 26, 140

Administrative tool, research as, *see* Applied research

Alford, L. P., 48

American Association for Labor Legislation, 30

American Bureau of Industrial Research, 25

American Federation of Labor, 21, 51, 52, 75

American Psychological Association, 66, 116

American Society of Mechanical Engineers, 47

Analysis, *see* Factor analysis; Regression analysis

Andrews, J. B., 30, 31

Applied research, 30–31, 37–55, 146–148, 154–158; *see also* Policy formation; Reformist research

Arbitration and conciliation, 22, 32, 52, 62, 80, 84, 104

Area Redevelopment Act, 89

Argyris, C., 95, 119, 149

Armour Automation Commission, 50, 91

Attitude studies, 49–50, 54, 65–68, 77, 94–98, 100, 141; *see* *also* Motivation; Organizational behavior

Automation, *see* Technological change

Bakke, E. W., 76, 95, 96, 119, 149

Barkin, S., 53

Barnett, G. E., 32, 62

Baxter, B., 116

Behavioral science, *see* Organizational behavior

Bendix, R., 105, 107, 150

Bingham, W. V., 48

Biographies, 75; *see also* Historical approach; Labor history; Oral history

Bradstreet's price series, 59–60

Brookwood Labor College, 8

Brown, J. D., 12

Bureau of Employment Security, 10, 88

Bureau of Labor Statistics, 10, 15, 19, 31, 43, 44, 45, 46, 53, 91, 102, 125

California Institute of Technology, 8, 48, 152

California, University of, 8, 73, 80, 88, 156

Campbell, A., 50, 124

Case study, 123–125; *see also* Study design

Center for the Study of Democratic Institutions, 99, 101

Chamberlain, N., 3, 76, 78, 79, 81, 113, 114

Chandler, Margaret, 79, 114

Chicago, University of, 8, 63, 64, 94, 99, 100, 135, 154

Child labor, 21, 22, 28, 41

Civil Rights Act, 45

Clothing Workers Union, Amalgamated, 51, 52–53

Collective bargaining, 31, 33–34, 42, 52, 62–63, 68, 76–77, 80, 81, 104–105, 108–109, 114–115

Columbia University, 9, 63, 73, 154

Commission on Industrial Relations, 27, 29, 31, 32, 34, 38, 64

Commons, J. R., 23, 25, 26, 27, 28, 29, 31, 37, 38, 42, 51, 57, 60, 61, 62, 63, 64, 65, 73, 74, 76, 78, 80, 82, 118, 124, 128, 135, 148

Communications, 6, 50, 94

Community studies, 75, 77; *see also* Environmental factors

Company unionism, 34–35, 42

Comparative studies, 124–125; *see also* Study design

Concepts, 113–115, 135, 136, 150–152

Conciliation, *see* Arbitration and conciliation

Congress of Industrial Organizations, 52, 75, 83

Consumer price index, 43; *see also* Prices

Contract studies, 44–45, 54; *see also* Applied research

Cornell University, 8, 9, 94, 102, 138

Corporate labor research, *see* Industrial research

Correlation analysis, 122

Cortner, R. C., 83

Dalton, M., 96, 126, 129

Data collection, 19–20, 60, 123, 163; *see also* Statistical surveys

Data processing, 152–153

Decision-making, 79, 81, 99, 109

Deductive theory, 24

Department of Labor, U.S., 10, 19, 21, 40, 41, 44, 60, 75, 140, 141; state, 10, 21, 22, 28, 59; *see also* Bureau of Labor Statistics *and other divisions*

Derber, M., 79, 105, 129

Dewey, J., 112, 161

Discrimination, 35–36, 45

Douglas, P., 60, 69, 118

Drucker, P., 96

Dunlop, J., 14, 77, 80, 81, 86, 103, 107, 118, 148

Economic development, 6, 103–104, 108, 142

Economics, 9; institutional, 7; laissez-faire, 24

Edelman, M., 78, 83, 85, 105, 115, 130

Education and training, 7, 8, 23, 27, 41, 90, 141; *see also* Industrial relations education

Eight-Hour Commission, 39, 40

Electrical Workers, Int'l. Brotherhood of, 51

Ely, R. T., 23, 24, 25, 26, 28, 57, 62, 82, 128

Empirical research, 12–13, 56–57, 81–82, 115–116, 143, 151–152
Environmental factors, 80, 109; *see also* Community studies
Equal Employment Opportunity Commission, 45

Factor analysis, 77
Federal Bureau of Labor, 23
Fiedler, F. E., 98
Field experiment studies, 127, 134, 135
Fitch, J. A., 29, 31
Foreign labor-management relations, 6, 40, 72, 79, 102–106, 141–142, 149–150; *see also* International comparative studies
Fringe benefits, 44, 50, 52
Fund for the Republic, 35

Game theory, 81
General Electric Co., 40, 50
General Motors Corp., 50
Government research, 9–10, 19–20, 22–24, 32, 37–46, 140–141, 143

Harbison, F. H., 76, 90, 103, 107
Harvard University, 9, 13, 48, 49, 65, 93, 99
Harwood Manufacturing Co., 68
Hawthorne study, 6, 49, 50, 67, 93, 127
Healy, J., 13, 79
Hedges, M., 51
Historical research, 9, 25–27; *see also* Biographies; Labor history; Oral history
Historical-institutional approach, 57, 60–63

Hollander, J., 56, 62
Hours of work, 22–23, 27, 30, 39, 40–41
Houser, J. D., 49, 65, 93
Hoxie, R. F., 32, 57, 63, 64–65, 99
Human relations in industry, 49, 77–78, 99–100
Hypotheses, *see* Theory

Illini City group, 76, 100, 119, 135
Illinois, University of, 8, 9, 54, 88, 98, 138, 139, 153
Incomes policy, 92, 105, 108; *see also* Wage stabilization
Individual research, 17, 134
Industrial Commission, U.S., 26, 31, 58; Wisconsin, 38
Industrial conflict, *see* Labor disputes
Industrial democracy, 26, 33, 79–80, 146; *see also* Industrial government; Labor union democracy
Industrial engineering, 7, 47–48
Industrial government, 61–62; *see also* Industrial democracy; Labor union democracy
Industrial Relations Counselors, 10, 50
Industrial relations education, 8–9, 138-139, 153–154, 159–164
Industrial Relations Research Assn., 11, 12, 88, 112, 131, 137, 140
Industrial relations theory, 11, 13–14, 80–82; *see also* Theory, role of
Industrial research, 10, 46–51, 143; *see also* Applied research

Industrial safety, 38; *see also* Workmen's compensation

Industrial society, 47–48, 65, 73, 106–108, 150

Industrial Workers of the World, 63, 64

Industry surveys, 42, 44, 53–54, 74–75, 76, 157; *see also* Applied research

Institutional approach, *see* Historical-institutional approach

Interdisciplinary research, 11, 15–17, 134–139, 142, 153–154; *see also* Multidisciplinary research

Int'l. Business Machines Corp., 50

International comparative studies, 6, 72, 102–106, 149–150; *see also* Foreign labor-management relations

Interpersonal relations, *see* Attitude studies; Motivation; Organizational behavior

Interpretive studies, 25

Investment in human capital, 36, 69, 90, 92, 144; *see also* Manpower planning

Job satisfaction, *see* Attitude studies

Johns Hopkins University, 23, 25, 56, 62, 99, 134

Joseph, M., 114

Kahn, R. L., 102, 149

Kelley, Florence, 28

Kellogg, P., 29

Kerr, C., 86, 103, 104, 107

Kornhauser, A., 65, 93

Labor and industrial relations, definition, 3, 12

Labor disputes, 6, 23, 31, 32, 46, 60, 63, 66, 75, 104, 132, 145

Labor folklore, 75

Labor history, 6, 23, 61, 72, 73–76, 148; *see also* Biographies; Historical research; Historical-institutional approach; Oral history

Labor legislation, 9–10, 23, 38, 82–83; protective, 31–32, 34, 146

Labor market, 6, 72, 84–92, 110, 120–122, 149; *see also* Labor mobility; Manpower planning

Labor mobility, 6, 7, 44, 84–85; *see also* Labor market; Manpower planning

Labor movement, 25, 33, 41, 61–63, 74–75, 104, 108–109

Labor organizations, *see* Labor movement; Labor unions

Labor relations theory, *see* Industrial relations theory

Labor turnover, 46, 48

Labor union democracy, 101–102; *see also* Industrial democracy; Industrial government

Labor union research, 10, 51–55, 143, 156–157

Labor unions: international affairs, 52; organization, 31, 32, 53–54, 60, 99, 109; policies, 63; political activities, 74, 76; structure, 34, 62–63; *see also* Organizational behavior

Labor-management relations, 5–6, 72, 76–82, 104, 109, 118–119, 123, 141, 148–149; *see also* Arbitration and conciliation; Collective bargaining; Foreign labor-management relations; Labor disputes

La Follette, R., 37, 38
Landrum-Griffin Act, 35, 147
Leadership, 98–99, 100–101; *see also* Organizational behavior
League for Industrial Democracy, 31
Lewin, K., 68, 120, 127
Lewis, H. G., 86, 114
Likert, R., 50, 97, 124, 149
Lipset, S. M., 101, 107
Livernash, E. R., 13, 79, 86
Loyola University, 8
Lynd, R. S., 17

McClellan committee, 35, 101
McGregor, D., 95–96, 97
McKersie, R. B., 81, 82, 114
Macdonald, R. M., 130
Machinists, Int'l. Assn. of, 52, 54, 75
Management organization, 6; *see also* Organizational behavior
Management research, *see* Industrial research
Management rights, 78–79, 113–114
Manly, B. M., 32, 33
Manpower Development and Training Act, 89
Manpower planning, 6, 7, 44, 46, 69, 90, 108; *see also* Investment in human capital
Massachusetts Institute of Technology, 8, 95
Massachusetts, University of, 8
Mayo, E., 6, 49, 65, 67, 78, 93, 94, 106
Mediation, *see* Arbitration and conciliation
Michigan State University, 9
Michigan, University of, 8, 50, 68, 73, 96, 102, 124, 154; Institute for Social Research,

96–98; Research Center for Group Dynamics, 68, 97; Survey Research Center, 50, 97, 124
Millikan, M., 157, 164
Mills, C. W., 94, 101, 106, 107, 150, 160
Minnesota, University of, 8, 9
Model-building, 68–70, 109, 122
Morale, *see* Attitude studies
Motivation, 47, 49, 68, 93–96, 98; *see also* Attitude studies; Organizational behavior
Multidisciplinary research, 16–17, 134–139, 142–143; *see also* Interdisciplinary research
Munsterberg, Hugo, 48, 57
Myers, C. A., 85, 103, 105, 107, 121

Nathan, R., 54
National Commission on Technology, Automation, and Economic Progress, 92
National Industrial Conference Board, 10
National Industrial Recovery Act, 41
National Labor Relations Act, 84
National Labor Relations Board, 42, 52, 83, 146, 147, 149
National Labor Union, 21–22
National Planning Assn., 76, 119, 123, 124, 135
National Recovery Admin., 41–42, 51
National War Labor Board, 42–43
New Deal, 34, 39, 41, 51, 75
New York State Commission on Employers' Liability, 30

Northrop, F. S. C., 160, 161

Occupations, 46, 85
Office of Manpower, Automation, and Training, U.S., 44
Office of Manpower Policy, Evaluation, and Research, U.S., 10, 45, 91
Older workers, 88–89
Operations research, 69
Oral history, 73; *see also* Biographies; Historical research; Labor history
Organizational behavior, 49, 64, 72, 77, 93–102, 108–109, 119, 120, 124–125, 126, 136–138, 141, 149; *see also* Attitude studies; Human relations; Labor unions; Management organization; Motivation

Parker, C., 63, 64–65
Parnes, H. S., 85, 115
Participant observation, 125–127
Pennsylvania, University of, 9, 80
Perlman, S., 32, 61, 102, 128
Placement, 48
Policy formation: private, 40, 157; public, 5, 11, 14–15, 24, 30–36, 39–46, 53, 72, 76, 82–84, 109, 142, 149, 164; *see also* Applied research; Reformist research
Poverty, 22, 35, 46
Power, 78
Presidential Railroad Commission, 91
President's Commission on Technology, Automation, and Economic Progress, 145

President's Council of Economic Advisers, 87
Prices, 22, 43, 46, 59–60, 87; *see also* Consumer price index
Princeton University, 8, 90
Printing Pressmen's Union, 53
Problem formulation, 112–122
Procter & Gamble Co., 49
Productivity studies, 44, 46, 60, 67–68, 75
Pulp & Sulphite Workers Union, 54
Psychological Corp., 49

Quantitative methods, 121–122, 128–130, 153

Railroad industry, 34, 39–40, 63
Reformist research, 21–36, 144–145, 158; *see also* Applied research; Policy formation
Regression analysis, 69, 122
Reynolds, L. G., 85, 86, 105, 121
Role theory, 97
Ross, A. M., 20, 46, 81, 86, 104

Safety, *see* Industrial safety
Sampling, 60, 77, 97, 124–125, 127, 141
Saposs, D. J., 31, 42, 103
Sayles, L. R., 78, 99, 127, 149
Scanlon plan, 95–96
Scientific management, 32, 46–47, 49, 51, 62, 64, 74
Scott, W. D., 48
Sears Roebuck & Co., 49, 50
Selection, 48
Selekman, B. M., 76, 78, 107
Slichter, S., 13, 32, 79
Social experimentation, 66–68
Social movements, *see* Industrial society
Social Science Research Council, 84, 121, 135

Social security, 34, 82

Social Security Administration, 10, 42, 52

Social workers, 28

Society for the Advancement of Management, 47

Society for the Psychological Study of Social Issues, 66, 132

Society to Promote the Science of Management, *see* Taylor Society

Sociopsychological approach, 63–66, 77

Senate Special Committee on Unemployment Problems, 89

Stanford University, 8

Statistical analysis, 127, 128–130; *see also* Statistical surveys

Statistical approach, 24, 58–60

Statistical surveys, 9–10, 19–20, 21–22, 42–43, 44, 52–53, 60, 75; *see also* Statistical analysis

Steelworkers of America, United, 53, 54

Strauss, G., 78, 99, 127, 149

Strikes, *see* Labor disputes

Study design, 122–128, 160–163; *see also* Case study; Comparative studies; Field experiment studies; Participant observation; Statistical surveys

Survey group, 28–29, 30, 31, 32

Survey research, *see* Statistical surveys

Sylvis, W., 21

Taylor, F., 46–47, 57, 66, 67

Taylor Society, 47

Teachers, American Federation of, 54

Team research, 17, 134–139; *see also* Interdisciplinary research; Multidisciplinary research

Teamsters, Int'l Brotherhood of, 52, 78, 101

Technological change, 7, 52, 62, 68, 91–92, 95, 108, 141, 145

Temporary National Economic Committee (Congress), 92

Testing, 48–49

Textile Workers Union, 52, 53

Theoretical model-building, *see* Model-building

Theory, role of, 115–122, 150–152, 162; *see also* Deductive theory; Empirical research; Game theory; Industrial relations theory; Role theory

Time study, 47, 66–67; *see also* Scientific management

Training, *see* Education and training

Twentieth Century Fund, 76, 88

Typographical Union, Int'l, 101

Ulman, L., 61, 74

Unemployment, 7, 22, 31, 34, 45, 46, 50, 87–92, 141; insurance, 38, 40–41

Unionization, *see* Labor movement

Union-management relations, *see* Labor-management relations

University Labor Education Association, 156

Values, 17–19, 130–134, 136, 145–146, 158, 160–161

Veblen, T., 63, 106

Vial, D., 156, 157
Vroom, V. H., 98

Wage and Hour and Public Contracts Division, 10, 42, 52
Wage Incentives, 47, 50
Wage stabilization, 6, 43; *see also* Incomes policy; Wages
Wages, 6, 22–23, 25, 40, 41, 43, 44, 46, 53, 59–60, 69, 75, 81, 84–88, 105; guaranteed annual wage, 54; *see also* Incomes policy; Wage stabilization
Wagner Act, 42, 83
Walton, R. E., 81, 82, 114
War Labor Board, 6, 15, 53
War Manpower Commission, 6, 44
Watkins, G., 41
Webb, S. & Beatrice, 56, 65
Weber, M., 106, 161
Western Electric Co., 67, 93, 127; *see also* Hawthorne study

Westinghouse Electric Corp., 50
Whyte, W. F., 76, 77, 94, 95, 100, 153
Wirtz, W. W., 20
Wisconsin, University of, 8, 9, 23, 25, 26, 27, 63, 73, 134, 138
Witte, E. E., 31, 82
Wolman, L., 32, 51, 60
Women in industry, 21, 23, 31, 69
Work methods, 47, 51, 66–67; *see also* Scientific management; Time study
Workers' participation in management, 103, 120; *see also* Industrial democracy; Industrial government
Working conditions, 22–23, 31, 40, 41, 49, 67
Workmen's compensation, 38, 48; *see also* Industrial safety
Wright, C. D., 22, 58, 59, 128

Yale University, 8, 95, 119